The PR practitioner's desktop guide

Caroline Black

HAWKSMERE

Published by Hawksmere plc

12-18 Grosvenor Gardens

London SW1W 0DH

www.hawksmere.co.uk

A CIP catalogue record for this book is
available from the British Library.

ISBN 1 85418 260 9

Printed in Great Britain by Ashford Colour Press.

Designed and typeset by Driftdesign
for Hawksmere.

Acknowledgements

I would like to thank my family, friends and colleagues whose encouragement spurred me on to finish this guide. Special thanks to the following, whose perceptive observations and suggestions considerably improved my early drafts:

The late Barbara Atkinson, Ian Beaumont, David Churchill, David Fanthorpe, Peter Hobday, Peter Holden, Kieran Knights, Jane Lyons, Alison Miles, Jonathan Reay, Amanda Riddle, Roger Sealey, Elizabeth Underwood, Nigel Wadlow, David Wells.

About the author

Caroline Black BA (Hons), MIPR, Dip coun

Caroline Black is a highly experienced communications consultant, writer, trainer, coach, mentor, facilitator, conference chair, lecturer and public speaker.

Her specialist areas include corporate, consumer, business-to-business and issues & crisis management communications. She began her career with the international advertising agency, D'arcy, switching to PR when she joined the in-house team at Guinness. She subsequently became a public relations consultant and was Board Director at Grayling, responsible not only for a number of large clients but also for both people and business development. She has worked for a wide range of clients and brands, including Sainsbury's, Investors in People UK, Ufi Ltd, Mobil, Mars, Pedigree Petfoods, Food from Britain, the European Union, British Gas, Smith & Nephew, Typhoo, Crookes Healthcare, the National Society for Epilepsy, the National Maritime Museum and the Rafsanjan Pistachio Producers Cooperative.

She set up her own consultancy, Caroline Black & Associates, in 2001.

Caroline is a member of the Institute of Public Relations and the Chartered Institute for Personnel and Development. She is also a qualified counsellor and an accredited officiant for the British Humanist Association.

Preface

Public relations is essential to managing and leading an organisation. It is particularly important to remember that protecting the brand, and protecting your good name is as significant an activity as safeguarding financial or human assets. Organisations who manage their PR professionally are in a much better position that those who let the PR function drift. It's a source of competitive advantage.

Consequently any organisation that wishes to succeed has public relations high on the strategic agenda. Public relations is recognised as an important management tool that enables an organisation to plan and to structure the way it communicates with its target audiences. In my view, internal communication between people working for an organisation and external communication with many influential stakeholder groups are of equal importance in ensuring an organisation meets its corporate objectives.

Public relations practice is changing all the time, propelled forwards by developments in communications technology. Public relations professionals need to keep up with the latest developments while at the same time understanding the established principles of good public relations practice.

The Public Relations Practitioner's Desktop Guide is a down-to-earth handbook, an essential for anyone involved in the public relations function for any type of organisation. It is jargon free, easy to read and accessible. Whether you are an in-house practitioner or a consultant working for clients, this book contains practical advice and suggestions, plus useful checklists and ideas for improving the way you work. It will also help you get to grips with today's fast moving media and communications channels.

For those new to public relations it is sure to become a well-worn and frequently consulted volume. It is the voice of the supportive coach, guiding and directing the less experienced. For old hands it's a refreshing reminder about best practice and a handy point of reference, the encouraging voice of the mentor and friend.

I hope you will find the Public Relations Practitioner's Desktop Guide a thoroughly useful addition to your bookshelf and a text you consult often.

Ruth Spellman
Chief Executive, Investors in People UK

Introduction

People not involved in the public relations business sometimes have curious ideas about what public relations is all about. Some of these impressions have been formed as a result of observing the antics of Edina and Bubbles in Absolutely Fabulous or having read about individuals' contracts with high profile publicists and agents that have resulted in front page 'kiss and tells' in the tabloids. Derogatory comments about 'PRs' from journalists and broadcasters imply that 'PR people' are lightweight, insincere, superficial social butterflies. Sound bites and spin doctors, photo stunts, lavish launches and lunches – all these give an impression that public relations is fluffy, frivolous and ultimately unnecessary.

Nothing could be further from the truth, as hard working public relations professionals will tell you, whether they are in-house practitioners or working as consultants. Public relations is now acknowledged to be a fundamental component in every intelligent organisation's strategy. There are important and serious objectives driving the public relations programme – to increase awareness, to improve reputation and trust, to create a point of difference, to educate, to reassure. When the going gets tough – in the event of a major issue or, worse, a crisis – the public relations function is central to the survival and recovery of organisations, and even governments.

In the twenty-first century, communication is instant. New media and the Internet have given us access to information 24 hours a day, 7 days a week, 365 days a year. This is the age of viral communication – a major news story breaks in London at 11.50 am and is world news at 12.00 midday. Fiercely protected reputations can be destroyed in moments. The organisation that engages in unethical practices or behaves irresponsibly and is dragged through the media mire will find its share price collapsed, its sales plummeting, its staff discontented and jaded. Every organisation must respond to these challenges – to build, protect and enhance its reputation – by being proactive, responsive, open and accessible in its communications with its key target audiences.

Thankfully the days when the Chief Executive's secretary 'looked after PR', often in the same way as she did the spider plants, are over. The public relations function now reports to senior management or to marketing and sometimes to both, particularly when products or services are involved. More and more frequently the senior management team includes an experienced public relations practitioner and board decisions are informed and influenced by the advice that that individual gives. Consultancies are used more effectively, to give objective advice and to provide additional resources. Evaluation is considered at the start of public relations planning and is no longer an afterthought.

It is hard but, for the most part, fascinating work. Those of us who are lucky enough to enter the public relations profession and then go on to make a career out of it will have the privilege of working, often at the very highest level, with talented entrepreneurs and chief executives of public and private sector organisations, committed and passionate campaigners in the voluntary sector, caustic, demanding but frequently witty journalists and photographers and energetic, creative and endearing colleagues. At least that has been my experience.

This guide has been written not only for those new to public relations but also for those who have been at it for some time. If you have just entered the profession or have taken on the responsibility for your organisation's public relations, I hope this guide will help you gain an understanding of some of the main principles and give you practical help and suggestions. These days the line between public relations and some other disciplines – like advertising, direct marketing, print, design, new media, sales promotions, event management and so on – is blurred. While it's always best to call in the experts for specific projects, it's important to have at least a basic understanding of these and so I have covered these briefly. I hope it will also complement any learning you undertake for recognised professional qualifications, such as the Institute of Public Relations' Diploma in Public Relations or the CAM Diploma.

If you have been working in PR for some time, please don't think I am teaching grandma to suck eggs. I have looked for concepts which represent best practice, gathered from many sources, from respected professionals, commentators and authorities. I hope that this guide will be a practical and useful sounding board, particularly in terms of the checklists, which may help save some time. On the other hand, you may disagree with some of what I have to say, in which case I would appreciate your views and comments for the next edition.

Finally it may seem strange for a text book to carry a dedication but this one does – it's for Joan and Bill Black, my mother and father, who worked so hard to make sure their children had the choices and opportunities they never had and enabled me to have the sort of career they could only dream of.

CONTENTS

Appendices 215

Icons

Throughout the Desktop Guide series of books you will see references and symbols in the margins. These are designed for ease of use and quick reference directing you to key features of the text. The symbols used are:

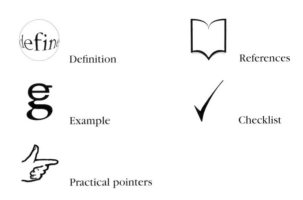

Definition

References

Example

Checklist

Practical pointers

chapter one

What is public relations?

Introduction

Relations… interpersonal relations, industrial relations, international relations.

People have a great many ideas about public relations and its purpose. PR not only stands for public relations as a function, it is also used as a noun to describe the public relations person, the 'PR'. PR has even been used as a verb ('I PR things'). PR has come to be understood by some as simply and only media relations. Some practitioners have dropped the term PR altogether and prefer to use the term 'communications' while others have opted for 'reputation management'. As an abbreviation, PR also stands for proportional representation. No wonder that there is uncertainty about what PR is – and what it is not.

Let's not confuse 'public' with '*the* public' either. In public relations practice, publics – or, to use less archaic terms, target audiences or stakeholders – are many and varied. An organisation can have many stakeholders – for example its own employees, customers and consumers, business partners, dealers and suppliers.

PR isn't publicity either. Publicists are often one-step away from showbiz promoters and use opportunistic, one-off stunts to gain media coverage, often by way of photo opportunities for the tabloid press.

While the good public relations practitioner promotes good, clear and simple communication, there can be some confusion about concepts in public relations. Like every other industry, public relations has its jargon, a patois that is an amalgam of management, marketing and media speak, impenetrable for the rookie and the outsider. There is a glossary at the end of this guide to help crack some of the industry jargon.

One thing is for certain – you can't choose to 'have' PR or not. An organisation can either take the initiative and acknowledge the powerful role that well managed, planned and proactive public relations can play in its development strategy or take a passive approach and sit back, leaving PR to fate. I know which sort of organisation I would rather work for and with.

Finally, as we will see when we discuss PR planning and evaluation, PR is a two-way street. A thorough understanding of the perceptions, views and opinions of the target audience(s) is vital to the development of an effective communications strategy.

Definitions

Public relations is...

'about reputation – the result of what you do, what you say and what others say about you.'

Public relations practice is...

'the discipline which looks after reputation – with the aim of earning understanding and support, and influencing opinion and behaviour.'

'it is the planned and sustained effort to establish and maintain goodwill and mutual understanding between an organisation and its publics.'

THE INSTITUTE OF PUBLIC RELATIONS (IPR)

'The method of defining messages and communicating them to targeted audiences in order to influence a desired response.'

THE PUBLIC RELATIONS CONSULTANCY ASSOCIATION (PRCA)

'Public relations is the management function that establishes and maintains mutually beneficial relations between an organisation and the publics on whom its success or failure depends.'

GLEN M BROOM, SAN DIEGO STATE UNIVERSITY

'Public relations practice is the art and social science of analysing trends, predicting their consequence, counselling organisation leaders and implementing planned programmes of action which will serve both the organisation's and the public interest.'

THE MEXICAN STATEMENT

CONFERENCE OF INTERNATIONAL PR PRACTITIONERS, MEXICO CITY 1978

'Public relations is the systematic attempt to influence people's beliefs, attitudes, opinions or behaviour towards an organisation, its products or services, or an issue or cause.'

THE IPR TOOLKIT • MICHAEL FAIRCHILD, IPR/PRCA1998 (REVISED 2001)

Is public relations propaganda?

From the 18th century Latin *'Sacra Congregation de Propaganda Fide'* (Sacred Congregation for Propagating the Faith)

Propaganda

Noun 1. The organised dissemination of information, allegations etc to assist or damage the cause of government, movement etc

Noun 2. Such information, allegations etc

Checklist

Use public relations to:

✓ Help build a positive reputation among an organisation's stakeholders.

✓ Contribute towards changing attitudes and perceptions and, ultimately, behaviour.

✓ Make people feel good about working in, or with, or for an organisation.

✓ Persuade potential employees that the organisation is 'right' for them.

✓ Educate stakeholders about the organisation and its products and services.

✓ Reach difficult or niche audiences precisely.

✓ Gain information about your stakeholders and your competitors, which will help your overall approach to marketing.

✓ Encourage debate and discussions about issues affecting the organisation and/or its sector.

✓ Help raise finance, attract investors and maintain confidence.

✓ Raise/increase awareness of the organisation, its products and services.

✓ Support corporate, sales and marketing strategies.

✓ Open new markets and prepare the way for and launch new organisations, products and services.

✓ Manage issues and crises.

Don't make assumptions – public relations will not:

✗ Change values, attitudes and opinions overnight – PR is long haul.

✗ Build a positive reputation when the organisation doesn't deserve it.

✗ Achieve objectives, which should be more appropriately set for other marketing disciplines, like advertising and sales promotion.

✗ Smother deserved complaint and criticism or act as a smokescreen for misdemeanour or malpractice – get your corporate act together.

✗ Guarantee media coverage – but good PR practice will increase your chances of coverage.

✗ Guarantee direct sales – although good PR practice will increase the likelihood of improved sales.

chapter two

A brief history of
public relations

Introduction

Public relations was born the moment the first organised group understood that it had a need to communicate with people – in other words it has been around since the dawn of civilisation.

In underdeveloped societies relationships were – and are – relatively simple. As societies become more sophisticated and multi-layered so the interplay of relationships becomes more intricate. This, together with the introduction of mass media in the nineteenth and twentieth centuries, led to the development of the theory and practice of public relations.

For the public relations practitioner, the roots of modern public relations illustrate clearly how public relations can be used to change perceptions, effect patterns of behaviour and accomplish far more than simply shifting products off shelves.

Then

The provision of information to precipitate change has been in evidence for thousands of years. Archaeological digs have unearthed shards of tablets written nearly 4,000 years ago which contain information for Mesopotamian farmers – handy hints and tips to help them improve productivity, including information on how to deal with field mice.

In the ancient world, the concept of public will and the power of pubic opinion was widely acknowledged as vital to any politician's success. The Caesars knew the importance of effective communication when they addressed the citizens of Rome in order to gain support and approval – from the Latin comes the expression *vox populi, vox Dei* – 'the voice of the people is the voice of God'. The fight organiser at the Coliseum knew he had to reach his potential customers with information about his product i.e. the dates and times of events. If he was canny he would also be aware that word of mouth accounts and reports of incredible shows and gladiators – in other words the positive reputation of the Coliseum – would be the ultimate persuasive pull, encouraging even greater numbers of eager Romans to seek out those dates and times. The early origins of showbiz PR – a-list personalities – drew the crowds then as much as they attract media attention now.

g

The first organised groups of persecuted Christians used the symbol of the fish for internal communications purposes, as a secret sign that only other Christians would recognise. It could be argued that this is one of the earliest examples of the use of a badge – a logo as corporate identity. Other examples are the use of crests in heraldry and of uniforms and regimental banners on the battlefield. Flags were the earliest corporate ID of a country, identifying one ship as friend and the other as foe.

There are many examples of early literature designed expressly for the purpose of creating understanding between an organisation and its target audiences, ranging from stone tablets, with hieroglyphics describing new laws, and 'wanted' posters, seeking bloodthirsty bandits, through to pamphlets, discussing new and challenging old political or social ideas, and leaflets, explaining how to create appetising family meals using turnips and parsnips or how to obtain rations during wartime.

With the industrialisation of society and the formation of many new organisations with political or commercial interests came the conscious understanding and widespread use of communications. The newspaper was the first medium through which messages were transmitted to large numbers of the public, while early forms of the in-house journal were used to inform staff and customer alike of developments within an organisation, or to deliver a sales message. Until the nineteenth century the press was owned by the establishment and relied on the government of the day for support. Investigative journalism was a phenomenon as yet unknown.

Media coverage reaching a specific readership and a defined and measurable audience became the goal for the public relations practitioner, indicating status, conferring kudos and implying editorial endorsement.

Developments in printing and the advent of new and mass media provided many more communications channels and routes to target audiences. Furthermore, periods of political, economic or social crisis precipitated faster developments in public relations practice and a more widespread use of public relations techniques. These factors moved public relations forward and helped to define it as the discrete and defined management practice we know today. The industry never stands still – the introduction of new media is and will continue to have a fundamental influence on the practice of public relations and political and economic factors will continue to shape the industry.

Successive governments have used public relations to effect changes in behaviour by explaining new policies relating, for example, to education and health. This continues to be a central feature of many government public relations programmes – for example the Department of Health campaign to reassure parents about the safety of the triple MMR (mumps, measles and rubella) vaccine and to encourage them to ensure their babies received the vaccine. Similarly the Department of Education and Skills lifelong learning campaign, which seeks to persuade adults to seek out courses and opportunities for self-development in order to improve their career prospects and achieve their personal potential.

Public relations was also extensively used to recruit in the public sector, the first major examples being for the army. Perhaps the most famous historical example is the army recruitment campaign that appeared during the First World War, memorable for the posters carrying Kitchener's image and the slogan 'Your country needs you'. This was specifically designed to communicate with able-bodied men and persuade them that their duty lay in signing up to the war effort. This was complemented by other information, arguably closer to propaganda. These uses of public relations have continued with contemporary campaigns attempting to attract teachers, police and even blood donors. Taken to the ultimate, public relations techniques can be used politically to transmit messages which are part of a propaganda campaign.

There are two main strands concerning the history of the development of contemporary public relations as an industry and management function. Uninterrupted by the Second World War with its attendant trading restrictions and rationing, the public relations industry in the US developed apace in the forties and fifties, alongside the growth of the advertising industry. Consequently public relations consultants and consultancies appeared in the States long before they appeared in the UK – the US has therefore claimed to be the originator of modern public relations practice.

In the UK advertising professionals who had been fully employed producing wartime propaganda, metamorphosised into the first professional public relations practitioners. They worked in-house for government and commercial organisations and as consultants in newly established public relations consultancies or branches of US consultancies which were beginning to expand as international networks.

Posters and packaging had been the main advertising media up until the forties. After this, advances in technology, particularly in communications, gave advertisers new and incredibly powerful routes to customers, enabling them to project their products into the home, most importantly via the TV screen. Vast numbers of new print titles – dependent on advertising for their growth and survival – were launched, designed to appeal to a society that was becoming ever more fragmented, with women emerging as a vital target audience with their own spending power and independence to make choices about the way they lived their lives and the way they spent their money. Manufacturers of fast moving consumer goods (FMCG) were among the first to use the new media to promote their products, from hairspray to cigarettes, chocolate bars to beer, toothpaste to toilet soap. As cars became more affordable, petrol and car advertising began to appear.

Public relations worked alongside advertising to create strong brands with perceived values and personalities, via consumer campaigns using media relations and editorial promotions, leaflets, exhibitions and demonstrations.

The last twenty years of the twentieth century saw enormous changes in the way we live and work. Against a political backdrop which believed the state should relinquish publicly owned utilities and industries and which encouraged entrepreneurialism, heavy industries were replaced by light industries, manufacturing declined and service industries boomed. As a concomitant, there was even greater need for business-to-business public relations to explain what was going on and to give companies a competitive edge. Deregulation was also a major driver for communications.

Likewise people were encouraged to become homeowners and to take responsibility for themselves, their families, their own health – enter mortgage lenders, building societies and banks, insurance brokers, financial services providers and healthcare companies as heavy users of public relations. Privatisation helped the general public to understand that they too could own stocks and shares. Corporate and financial public relations became a vital part of the communication strategy for most successful organisations.

After a series of high profile incidents and health scares, organisations slowly but surely began to realise that reputation is a very valuable item on the balance sheet and that a lost reputation is rarely found. Oil companies, drugs companies, governments and charities added issues and crisis management to the management agenda.

In the early days PR was learnt on the job. Most professionals had worked their way through the ranks. But towards the end of the twentieth century professional qualifications were available to the PR practitioner which started to contribute towards raising the status and reputation of the industry as a whole.

Now

Alongside political and economic change has been the development of new communications across the globe. PCs at work and at home, the Internet and e-mails, mobile phones, micro-technology and ever-cheaper technology have changed how individuals behave. Children have televisions and PCs in their bedrooms, families are less likely to eat together or to eat the same meal. Workers in multinational corporations communicate across cultures instantly and must be 'globile' – able to move to and work in any country if the business demands it. The international brand is king and pan-European/global campaigns are commonplace.

At the same time anti-capitalists and greens are organising themselves – ironically communicating via electronic media – to protest against globalisation, human and animal exploitation and environmental damage caused by governments and corporations all over the world.

The media is fragmented. More magazines come and go every year with growing numbers having their own websites. A plethora of cable and satellite channels offering a huge choice are steadily changing the way we view television and listen to radio. Online entertainment is taking off, with penetration increasing among all age groups and social classes.

Opportunities for media relations have never been greater, while at the same time the world has got wise to the fact that public relations is a powerful tool. This includes people who work in the media who know organisations want airtime and column inches, and increasingly look for reciprocal deals through advertising, sponsorship and joint activities. The old interdependency between media and advertiser is still there.

For the PR professional, PR has become a mature marketing discipline and is now a central feature of many successful companies' strategies. It is ranked alongside – or in place of – advertising and has achieved professional status, with vocational training and recognised qualifications. Evaluation means that the positive contribution made by PR to the organisation's communication strategy can now be measured and appreciated.

Tomorrow

Even if they are spending more time looking at computer screens and chatting on mobile phones, people are still reading, watching television, driving cars, buying groceries (even if they are delivered to the door), enjoying a pint of lager, going on holiday, buying their own homes and investing and putting money aside into pensions. Businesses will always need to trade with each other, companies are always looking for investors, voluntary organisations are still seeking to raise funds and put their cause on the map, and government departments still need to get policy and educational messages across.

What is changing is technology and the way organisations communicate with their target audiences via an increasing number of sophisticated and direct routes. The PR practitioner must keep abreast of developments in the media world.

In the future, the PR practitioner may be the most likely candidate to manage any ethics committees within an organisation, charged with interrogating corporate behaviour in order to protect corporate reputation. It is already a demanding role – PR at the highest level is now and will continue to be a 24 hours a day, 365 days a year job. Systematic evaluation is a major element in most organisations' PR plan and this trend will continue using ever more sophisticated tools. With faster technology the numbers of those employed in public relations could fall – conversely the growing importance of public relations may mean that numbers employed in the profession will increase.

One thing is for certain – public relations is here to stay.

Timeline – the history of communication

▶ **Early civilisation**

- Cuneiform writing in Mesopotamia
- Archaeological evidence of information campaigns
- Paper invented in China c100AD

▶ **1450**

- Gutenberg's printing press

▶ **1477**

- Caxton sets up press in Westminster

▶ **1480**

- First known circular for advertising purposes – Germany

▶ **Middle ages**

- Public proclamations, posted bulletins and announcements for political and religious purposes
- 1565 – first pencil

▶ **1643**

- Publication of *New England's First Fruits* – first known public relations bulletin produced for fundraising purposes, printed in London for the US
- American War of Independence – the first coherent campaign to change opinion and legislation using classic public relations techniques e.g. the formation of a campaigning group (The Sons of Liberty), staged events (the Boston Tea Party), symbols (the Liberty tree) and slogans ('Taxation without representation is tyranny')

► **1665**

- Publication of first periodical other than a newspaper – *Journal des Scavans*

► **1754**

- *Yorkshire Post* launched

► **1785**

- *The Times*, founded as the *Daily Universal Register*

► **1809**

- British Treasury appointed its first press spokesman

► **1814**

- Steam powered cylinder press first used to print *The Times* in London

► **1820-30s**

- 1821– *Manchester Guardian* founded (renamed *The Guardian* in 1959)
- Rise of democracy in the US and use of media to convey political messages
- 1837 – *ABC Telegraph* invented by Cooke and Wheatstone
- 1837 – *Northern Star* (Leeds) regional paper launched

► **1840**

- First postage stamps – Rowland Hill

► **1850s**

- Information campaigns enticing settlers from the East to the West coast of America including Burlington Railroad's campaign of 1858
- 1851– Invention of plate camera
- 1854 – Post Office recognises the necessity to explain services to the public
- 1855 – *Daily Telegraph* founded

▶ **1870s**

- 1870 – Invention of the typewriter

- 1876 – Invention of the telephone by Alexander Graham Bell

▶ **1890s**

- 1894 – Marconi sends first radio waves

- 1896 – Launch of *Daily Mail*

▶ **1910s**

- 1911 – Air mail adopted

- 1912 – Lloyd George organises a team of lecturers to explain the first pension scheme for the elderly

- 'Your country needs you' poster campaign

- 1918 – Launch of the *Express*

▶ **1920s**

- 1920 – First radio station Pittsburgh, USA

- 23 February 1922 – first edition of *Good Housekeeping*

- Crystal sets to listen to radio broadcasts

- 1926 – Empire marketing board campaign to promote fruits and other products imported from the British Empire

- 1926 – John Logie Baird demonstrates television for the first time

- 1926 – Royal Charter awarded to the British Broadcasting Corporation

▶ **1930s**

- Valve radios

- 1936 – First television broadcasts from Alexandra Palace, North London

- 1938 – Invention of the ball-point pen and photocopier

- Development of all-electronic television

► **1940s**

- Wartime propaganda using radio and educational campaigns using posters and print
- 1943 – Invention of circuit board
- Concept of the mobile phone appears
- 1946 – Invention of the computer
- 1947 – Invention of the transistor
- 1948 – Institute of Public Relations (UK) and Public Relations Society (USA) formed

► **1950s**

- Many women's magazines launched
- 1950 – Diner's Club – first credit card
- 1953 – First colour television broadcast
- 1955 – Commercial TV launched in the UK
- 1954 – First transistor radio built
- 1956 – First video recorder
- 1959 – Invention of microchip

► **1960s**

- 1962 – First communication satellite
- 1963 – First cassette recorder
- 1964 – First word processor
- Development of the Internet by the Pentagon

► **1970s**

- 1974 – Invention of the bar code
- 1978 – First personal computer
- 1979 – Sony walkman
- Internet developed
- Mobile phones begin to appear

▶ **1980s**

- 1980 – Post-it notes appeared

- 1982 – First smart card and CD player

▶ **1990s**

- 1990 – Videophone

- World Wide Web developed by European scientists

- Voice recognition software for PCs

- Mobile phone saturation in UK

▶ **21st Century**

- 11 September 2001 – Terrorist attacks in the US – instant news across the globe

chapter three

The public relations practitioner

Introduction

Public relations is a highly competitive business, hard to break into and hard work when you get there. Professional standards are improving all the time, with the introduction of vocational public relations and communications diplomas and degrees. The job itself is getting more and more demanding. 'Why did I choose this as a career', I have sometimes asked myself, 'when I could have been a florist?'

The answer is simple – this is a fascinating and challenging industry, no two days are the same and, most importantly, you can help make a real and positive difference, sometimes in small ways and sometimes in very dramatic ways, sometimes for start-ups, sometimes for major plcs, sometimes for marginalised and disenfranchised groups. You can write a press release alerting the media about a new strain of meningitis in the morning and manage a corporate event for an energy company that evening; work with the chief executive of a major charity on a crisis plan on a Thursday and advise a new media entrepreneur on a Friday, lead a press trip round a state of the art frozen pea factory in York one week and discuss the versatility of the pistachio nut as a food ingredient in Tehran the next.

I have worked with hundreds of PR professionals over the years – in-house practitioners, consultancy teams and freelance consultants – as a consultant, as a colleague and as a client. When I run training courses or talk at seminars, I am frequently asked, 'What does it take to be a good PR professional? Have I got it?' In this chapter we will look at the personal qualities you need, the skills you will have to acquire, the routes into PR and how to look after yourself when you're holding down what can be a very demanding role indeed.

A word of advice – always be scrupulously honest with yourself. If you know in your heart of hearts that you don't have what it takes – or that you have lost it – don't keep banging your head against the wall. This is not failure. Keep on reassessing where you are, talk to your boss, try a different sort of PR job, perhaps in a specific sector or industry, get some training to refresh yourself or to learn new skills. Move on if you need to, to check that it's not just *this* job that's preventing you from realising your potential. And change direction if you must. There is nothing sadder than someone who feels trapped because they don't feel they can do anything else or because they know they can't go any further.

Qualities and skills

There is no doubt that effective PR practitioners need a number of both personal qualities and professional and business skills and that these are entirely different and separate from any consideration of academic achievement. In HR speak these might be referred to as 'core competencies'.

Some people believe that personal qualities are innate while professional skills can be learnt. What is certainly true is that many of the professional skills build on personal qualities. I would contend that they are all relevant whether you are working in-house or as a consultant. There are one or two more business orientated skills which are specific to the consultant.

Check out how you match up. While you don't necessarily have to have every one of these qualities or be accomplished in every skill, the more you have the more effective a practitioner you are likely to be.

If you are responsible for recruiting or appraising people who will be working as public relations practitioners - including appointing consultants - these checklists will help by giving some ideas for creating or updating job descriptions and appraisal systems.

Personal qualities of the effective public relations practitioner

Good communicator

An absolute basic. Of course you can develop specific communication skills but you must be interested in and gain pleasure from expressing yourself verbally and in the written form. You will also need to be able to communicate with a wide variety of people, from consumer or customer to senior colleague or client, so the ability to adapt both approach and language and to empathise is fundamental.

Perspective/sense of humour

You'll need it, particularly when dealing with difficult people or difficult situations. A sense of humour helps the communication process, breaks the ice, puts you on the level and defuses explosive situations. Most of the time what seems so important today is likely to seem pretty trivial in a year's time. And don't beat yourself up if something goes wrong - make sure you learn if you make a mistake.

Calm under pressure

Stress is inherent in most jobs and it's no different in PR, particularly if there are deadlines to be met or crises to deal with. Sometimes pressure is self-generated (especially if you are a perfectionist), sometime it comes from external forces (for example if a crisis occurs which throws everything into chaos). Regardless of the circumstances and source you need to be able to function effectively and you will often have to take a leadership role.

Creative

While best practice in PR has perhaps led to 'prescription' solutions in terms of processes and even tactics, the campaigns that always work best are those which have been given a truly creative spin and which stand out from the crowd. Some PR practitioners are inevitably more creative than others, although you can work at this to increase your creative capacity. If this is one of your innate talents, nurture it and use it wisely – it will always be needed in a competitive environment.

Organised

The PR practitioner usually finds him/herself working on a number of projects with a number of colleagues, consultants, clients, suppliers and media at any one time. Plus he/she needs to have the ability to create and use schedules, critical paths and timing plans so that the work actually gets done on time.

And while you may be one of those people who works best with a workspace that looks like a bomb's hit it, your team members will thank you for self-management that enables them to locate important documents if you are off-site or off sick. Time management skills can be learnt but an organised approach to work is a considerable plus point.

Willingness to learn

When you start it is useful to think of yourself as a sponge, absorbing all you learn on the job. Infact never stop being a sponge – each time you are faced with a new situation you should be prepared to learn from it. In this way your professional judgement sharpens and your advice to colleagues and clients becomes based on experience and analysis.

Curious

This is a quality possessed by the best journalists, who dig deeply to find the truth and the story. In the same way you need to be curious about your industry, your product, and your organisation. This is especially true when you are planning your PR strategy and when critical interrogation of briefs and rigorous auditing of information is vital.

Warm/approachable/down to earth

PR practitioners are often called upon to build relationships with a wide number of people, both inside and outside the organisation. While there are some stand-offish and rather superior PR folk, the best have a 'way with people' that invites people to talk to them, to tell them what is going on, to give them the story, to tell them the truth and to give them what they need to do their job more effectively.

Confident

Confidence breeds confidence and your colleagues and clients will feel more assured and comfortable with a confident professional. The downside is that real confidence comes with knowing your subject and this often builds over the years, when you know you have 'been there, done that' and can advise accordingly. However, you can give assurance by being positive and by being assertive. While you may not have all the answers, you can consult with superiors, peers and external consultants.

Focused

Because there is a lot of juggling, you need to be able to concentrate on specific issues and not be distracted by the one hundred and one things that are going on at the same time. You need to be able to think clearly to arrive at quality solutions and ideas.

Practical

Much as I hate overworked clichés, PR is not rocket science and the best campaigns and programmes are based on a limited number of objectives, a sparky creative strategy and eminently practical tactics that work. There is no point putting up a concept if it just can't be translated into practical action and the PR practitioner must be able to select what will – and reject what won't – work.

Energy

You need energy and stamina for this sort of work. PR practitioners are often on call 24/7, particularly given round the clock broadcasting. You may be at a sponsored event until two in the morning and up again at six to run a stand at a conference. You need to be able to perform regardless and to always have a smile on your face.

Enthusiasm

Sometimes a task or a brief will match your personal interests and enthusiasms (for example, promoting Spanish wines). But sometimes you may be faced with a brief that doesn't have the same immediate appeal (for example, presenting a new design of sewerage pipe to water companies). This sort of situation is encountered perhaps more often by consultants than in-house people. However, by attacking a problem with enthusiasm and gusto, it can often become incredibly interesting and can even become a personal passion.

Assertive

The PR practitioner is never aggressive or passive. A healthy assertiveness is important and will help you do your job more effectively and give yourself some space. Again this can be learnt, so get yourself on a workshop if you need help.

Tough

While there will be highs in a career in PR, there are always lows too – the fabulous photocall with a flavour of the month celebrity that didn't attract one national press photographer, the press trip that resulted in one piece in a trade press title, the pitch you worked on late every night for a month and lost, the client with whom you just can't gel. That's the nature of the business. You need to have, or acquire, a reasonably thick skin.

Professional and business skills for the effective public relations practitioner

Integrity

The more PR professionals behave professionally, the better for the industry as a whole and all of us who work in it as individuals. It's about our reputation, as communicators of the truth. While we are charged with presenting our organisations in the best light, we must also take responsibility for purveying the truth and we must always be able to feel we are working with integrity.

Let's look at the skills you will need to acquire – many of these skills are covered in more detail later in this guide, some meriting a dedicated chapter.

Public relations essentials

It is useful to grasp the fundamentals of PR early on in your career. Induction, coaching, mentoring and on-the-job experience will give you much of this and this guide will help. There are also starter training courses available which may be worthwhile considering, depending on your needs and budget.

Planning and evaluation skills

Key in terms of making sure PR is accountable and measurable.

Writing skills

If there is one single thing PR people do a huge amount of, it's writing. Releases, features, reports, photocaptions, copy, speeches, letters… the list goes on. Writing is as much about grammar, spelling, form and style as it is about content. Journalists, who are after all professional writers, are immensely irritated by poor writing skills exhibited by PRs and cite the receipt of badly written releases as a reason to ignore or, worse, lampoon an organisation.

Presentation skills

There is often a lot of presentation work in public relations, perhaps more if you are a consultant and pitch for business on a regular basis. Sometimes you may have to present to small groups, sometimes to very large groups. At the least you may have to make announcements at events and use your voice effectively.

Media relations skills

Best practice for handling the media, creating coverage and handling media interviews. The practitioner must know how to target and who to target with media stories, must be able to distinguish between news and non-news, must know what makes an effective photo and must be competent enough to handle a press conference (if required), or just one difficult journalist.

Consultancy skills

Whether in-house, working as an internal consultant to colleagues, or in consultancy, working for fee-paying clients, you will need to develop consultancy skills. There are differing consulting styles, appropriate to different situations and again there are training courses to help develop these skills.

Client handling skills

How to relate to a client and develop long-term and fruitful relationships. This may include listening skills, questioning techniques, negotiation, new business pitching and auditing client satisfaction levels.

IT skills and e-communications

PR practitioners need to be well versed in all new developments which affect the way we communicate with each other. This means not simply knowing how to surf the net but also appreciating the effect new media is having on the target audience, understanding how to use these new channels effectively in public relations programmes and using these new tools to enhance and protect the organisation's reputation.

Issues and crisis management

In every organisation, sector and industry there is the potential for reputations to be damaged as a result of an issue going live (such as informed consent relating to organ retention for research purposes) or a crisis occurring (such as a train derailment which results in loss of life). Every PR practitioner should have at least a basic understanding of planning for these eventualities.

Reputation management

At the heart of every definition of public relations is the notion of reputation. Practitioners should develop an intellectual understanding about the importance of reputation; how it is created, what it is worth on the corporate balance sheet and how it is lost.

Budget management and profitability

On a practical level budget management is vital for both in-house and consultancy practitioners. Profitability is mainly an issue for the consultant who will be expected to deliver profit to the consultancy while still giving high levels of client satisfaction.

Project management

Most PR programmes have many component parts and the PR practitioner needs project management skills in order to deliver on time and within budget.

Specialist sector skills

Healthcare, public affairs, consumer PR and so on – each has characteristics of its own and the specialist practitioner will need to develop the knowledge and awareness of what is best practice in his/her field. This must include an understanding of legal parameters and codes of conduct.

Business strategy skills

Financial strategy, people strategy and marketing strategy – all are important for the consultant who is either managing his/her own business or who is working in a larger consultancy. The skills of a small business owner/manager are a good starting point – a part-time or flexible learning MBA might be considered.

Marketing skills

Because the PR strategy should be aligned to other communications strategies, the practitioner benefits from an understanding of other marketing disciplines. Additionally the consultant may be charged with the responsibility to market his/her own organisation.

In-house and consultancy

In-house PR

For one company, government department or organisation exclusively, closely aligned to the management and providing a service to the whole organisation.

The in-house PR may also be subcontracting to and then managing consultancies, so he/she may be a client as well as a PR practitioner.

The in-house practitioner may be working alone, be part of a small team, work in association with colleagues in other locations in the UK or abroad or be part of a huge department, servicing a large organisation.

In-house suits those who want to work in one organisation or industry and who want to specialise in a subject. It is also a little more likely to suit people who want to be able to manage their lives in terms of what hours they might work or where they might be from one week to the next as most in-house jobs – though by no means all – are governed by the organisation's employment terms and conditions which may include flexitime.

Consultancy PR

Working for one or more clients in a consultancy which may be generalist or may offer expertise in one particular sector e.g. consumer PR.

The consultant needs to be able to be something of an entrepreneur too as building business – by winning and keeping clients – is vital in consultancy.

Consultancy teams are made up of board directors, account directors, account managers and account executives, with account teams constructed to reflect the needs of the client and the size of the budget.

Because of the nature of consultancy, the life better suits people who are able to and ideally who want to move around from subject to subject, industry to industry, location to location. Hours vary, given that the consultant is offering a service to clients who may need support at unsocial times including evenings and weekends. Because consultants usually work for more than one client he/she will need to juggle time and may need to spend considerable time travelling from one location to another or away from home.

Ways into the business

People get into the public relations business in a variety of ways mainly:

- On graduate recruitment schemes – particularly if the graduate has qualifications in PR or marketing

- By migrating from one industry to another – for example, journalists and marketing consultants switching, nurses moving to healthcare public relations

- By migrating from consultancy to in-house and vice versa

- By taking on public relations as another responsibility – for example, as part of the marketing role

- By entering as a PA or secretary, gaining on the job training and then promotion.

Qualifications, training and Continuing Professional Development

- There are a number of universities and colleges that offer degrees in public relations and marketing either as full-time or part-time courses. Information on courses is available from *learndirect* on 0800 100 900.

- The Communications, Advertising and Marketing Foundation (CAM) offers the well-established CAM Diploma, which is recognised and supported by the industry.

- The IPR now offers a vocational diploma suitable for those embarking on a career in public relations. The IPR also launched its Continuing Professional Development (CPD) scheme for experienced practitioners in 2000, designed to encourage experienced practitioners to learn new skills and consider current best practice. This is also supported by the PRCA.

- Other reputable organisations, such as Hawksmere and Communications Skills Europe, offer an extensive selection of tailored courses and workshops for the PR practitioner, covering all aspects of the job including specialisms such as public affairs and financial public relations. Some of these have been approved by the IPR as they offer training and development modules which meet the CPD standards.

- Like most industries, the most common type of personal development is on the job training.

- More and more organisations, including PR consultancies, are committing to achieving the Investors in People Standard. This is a sound framework for improving organisational performance through people development. For the public relations practitioner, this can only be a good thing – our industry moves incredibly fast and we need continuing training at every stage of our careers.

It's all in a day

I have been asked 'so what do you actually **do**?' As mentioned in the introduction, the job is infinitely varied and, particularly as you become more experienced, you will find that no day is the same as the next. But if you want to explain to a rookie what might be in store for them in terms of a list of tasks they might be expected to complete during the working week, it would probably include some or all of the following:

- Daily media monitoring – web media, press, TV, radio, relevant chatrooms and newsgroups – relaying it to those who need to know and advising on what action to take as a result of media coverage

- Updating the media pages on the organisation's website

- Researching media contacts and updating contact details

- Contacting the media

- Writing – releases, feature material, background information, brochures and leaflets, letters, newsletters and reports

- Managing creative work – photography, design and print

- Managing presentations and events – launches, conferences and meetings

- Briefing spokespeople or acting as spokesperson

- Communicating with and updating colleagues/clients

- Planning future projects and programmes.

Looking after yourself

It's a tough job and there will be demands made of you which might not be made of others. In-house practitioners may be expected to take responsibility for tasks which do not fall into any other neat category and so are lumped under PR. Consultants may have to juggle a number of clients, each of whom are making demands on you at the same time, while working on two new business pitches and updating the consultancy website. Whether in-house or consultant, another frequent cause of tension is the naïve expectation that the PR practitioner's main or even sole responsibility is to deliver vast quantities of positive media coverage, whatever the story, whatever the day of the week. The management of issues and crises make particular demands on PR practitioners, in terms of time and tension levels. Just running a good press office might mean you are on call 24 hours a day, 7 days a week.

You need to look after yourself, physically and mentally. Here are ten helpful tips to keep you sane:

1. Get enough sleep

It's easy to work hard, play hard and think that four or five hours will suffice. You need to be alert and on the ball in this job. Performance falls off if you are sleep deprived. If you lie awake in the middle of the night worrying about something then get up, have a glass of water and write down what's bothering you – but if insomnia is a persistent problem then it may be time to take a long hard look at the way you are working and be prepared to make a change if you need to.

2. Drink lots of water

It's too easy to get so engrossed in your work that you forget to rehydrate. Get a water dispenser for the office or buy yourself a filter jug and keep it on your desk at work. Travel with a bottle of still mineral water in your bag. Drink a glass of water as soon as you get up, one before lunch and supper. Replace tea and coffee at meetings with water. Choose still rather than carbonated water, it's better for your stomach.

3. Watch the alcohol consumption

In this sociable business, it's easy to find yourself drinking almost every day, with colleagues after work, with clients or consultants at lunch, with journalists, at events, at receptions. It becomes a habit. You don't need to stop but it is a good idea to stick to recommended safe levels (21 units a week for men and 14 units for women) and to try to replace alcohol with water or soft drinks whenever you can.

4. Eat often but lightly

So you don't suffer from the after lunch droop or morning after paralysis – keep a fruit bowl on your desk and snack healthily to keep energy levels high.

5. Take it easy with technology

Take regular breaks away from the PC screen. Let your eyes refocus and do some stretching exercises. No one really knows whether there are any long-term side effects from using mobile phones – but the frustration of using them in terms of reception quality and having to listen to other people shouting into them puts them high on the list of stress makers, even if they do offer the convenience of communication anytime, anywhere.

6. Learn about time management

Apply any helpful hints and tips to buy time for life after and outside work.

7. Walk – everywhere

Up stairs, from floor to floor, from office to office, from the station to the meeting, from the meeting to the station. You may think that the taxi will get you there quicker, but traffic is so congested these days the walk will take you only a fraction longer and gives you time to think, to breath and give your legs a stretch. On business overseas, especially on long haul flights, move about if you can or at least stand and bend and flex your legs every hour.

8. Get involved with one sport as a player

It's not only good for you, it may also be a good opening gambit for conversation on social occasions and, if it's a team game, it gives you an excuse for a social get together with clients or colleagues.

9. Get a life outside of PR

Don't forget your partner/family/friends. Put birthdays and anniversaries in your diary, take holidays, don't take work home unless it really is an emergency, get a dog and take it for walks after work, get a cat and stroke it (good for the blood pressure). Be multi-dimensional and get passionate about something – try volunteering for a local charity or get involved with a local community project, take up a new hobby, learn a new skill online, just do something you haven't done before and keep yourself interested and interesting.

10. Stop beating yourself up – about anything and everything

This is especially true if you work for an organisation where issues and/or crisis management are at the fore or if you work with colleagues or clients who are particularly demanding. Give yourself a break – a bit of time to think – or not to think – a treat, a space and reward yourself for working hard. Pat yourself on the back when you have done a good job and put mistakes down to experience. Learn to let go when you have done your bit. Don't carry guilt, regret or anger around with you. And be assertive when you need to be.

Finally, don't take yourself or PR too seriously – sure, it's an important job but it is just a job in the end. Few of us see PR as a vocation or have so little else in our lives that we want to spend every hour of every day doing it or talking about it. You could just get a little boring or come over as a little obsessive. Don't take this advice if you are ambitious to become one of those people whose names are synonymous with the business or if you want to be filthy rich – in which case knuckle down, focus on the business, get your name about and network at every conceivable opportunity.

Checklist

✓   Make a list of personal qualities and professional skills – measure how you are doing at regular intervals.

✓   Use this list during appraisals and discussions about your career development.

✓   Seek out training and development opportunities to sure up weak areas or to acquire new skills.

✓   When you switch job or get promoted review your development needs.

✓   Make sure you have an up-to-date job description.

✓   Investigate whether a mentor or personal coach would be helpful – have an initial meeting to see how it might benefit you.

✓   Consider joining the IPR. If you are already a member make full use of the organisation for networking and personal development.

✓   Look for easy ways to get fitter – just walking up the stairs instead of taking a lift will help.

✓   Learn how to relax and get things into perspective.

chapter four

Ethical and legal issues for the public relations practitioner

Introduction

Given that the objectives of public relations are concerned with the building and maintaining of reputation and the proactive propagation of positive messages, there is a need for codes of conduct which set store on honesty and integrity within the industry. We must of course also work within the bounds of the law.

The industry has recognised codes of conduct. If you are a member of either the IPR or the PRCA, it is incumbent upon you to adhere to these codes. Even if you are not a member of either body, I would urge you to familiarise yourself with the codes. You will then know what to expect if you are working with PR professionals who are members of these organisations. The codes raise awareness of some of the issues regarding standards of behaviour in the industry. There will always be individuals who profess they are public relations professionals but whose *modus operandi* is somewhat outside of these codes. If you are working with any individual or company, as employee or client, make sure you are satisfied that third parties adhere to these codes or are members of the professional bodies.

Public relations practitioners also have to take into account aspects of the law that affect the particular industry they are working in. Public affairs, financial public relations and healthcare are perhaps the three specialist areas most strictly regulated in this way.

This chapter outlines some of the ethical and legal issues the PR practitioner should become familiar with, but remember laws and codes of conduct change. *Always go back to the authorities for the most up-to-date legislation and versions of codes of conduct or practice –* increasingly, these are available on websites.

Codes of conduct

The two codes that define standards for the industry as a whole are:

- The Institute of Public Relations Code of Professional Conduct (www.ipr.org.uk)

- The PRCA Professional Charter for Consultancies (www.prca.org.uk)

They are reviewed periodically and are posted on the relevant organisation's website. Versions of each obtained at the time of writing are included in the appendices.

Complaints against the press

The Press Complaints Commission was set up in 1991 – this acts as a channel for those who believe that they have been treated unfairly or that their privacy has been invaded to bring complaints against the media. Contact the Commission for more information.

As far as television and radio are concerned, the Broadcasting Standards Commission investigates complaints. If you feel you have been misrepresented in the making of a TV programme consult the ITC code of conduct or the BBC Producers Guidelines.

Contracts

All PR practitioners need to understand the importance of contracts. We engage in work with many third parties and protection in the form of a contract is vital for all parties involved. The main relationship requiring a contract is that between client and consultancy. But other relationships will require contracts too – for example, with a third party who is sponsoring one of your projects, a photographer who is responsible for your photo-library or a new media specialist who is designing your website. Contracts should cover:

- Terms and conditions – related to the programme of work

- Scope of the contract – the detailed plan of action with milestones and timelines (not carved in stone! This must be flexible to allow for amendment and improvement along the way)

- Key performance indicators – detailing expected servicing levels

- Financial arrangements – what is being billed, what it covers and what it does not cover, when it will be billed and the purchase ordering system

- Approvals and authorities – to sign off work and to commit monies

- Copyright – what belongs to the third party and what belongs to you

- Confidentiality

- Insurance and liability

- Notice periods – for termination of contract or review (up or down) of fee and service levels.

The contract sets and manages expectations and protects both parties in the event of misunderstanding or dispute. It is a useful and 'live' document, not 'just a formality' nor a stick to beat the other party with. Always get something in writing – these days a handshake is never enough. Get your legal department or a solicitor to clear your contract and read all the small print. The PRCA has a useful standard contract for its members.

Competitions, raffles and reader offers

PR practitioners often get involved with these sorts of activities to promote their organisation, products or services. These are covered by the Betting, Gaming and Lotteries Act 1963, which should always be consulted if planning this type of activity.

Competitions

- Include the rules or information about where to get copies of the rules.

- Competitors must be required to use their judgement.

- Entries must be fairly judged.

- Draws are allowed in certain cases.

Raffles

- Check local by-laws.

- Print the name and address of the organiser on tickets sold to the general public.

Sales promotions

- Get advice and information from the Institute of Sales Promotion.

Defamation

PR is a competitive business and your organisation wants more favourable coverage than your competitor. There may be occasions when, in order to gain the high ground or score points, your organisation contemplates taking on or challenging a competitor.

Written or oral statements might be made which could be construed as slanderous or libellous because they are:

- Defamatory

- False (unless proved to the contrary)

- Refering to a third party

- Made known to at least one person other than the third party.

Don't get caught in a slanging match unless you are absolutely sure of your ground, have sound evidence and are unquestionably in the right. Any action which involves a legal battle is bound to be expensive, not only in terms of legal fees but also because of the knock-back effect on your reputation if you are found to be in the wrong.

Slander – defamation in some transient form as by spoken words, gestures, performances.

Libel – the publication of defamatory matter in permanent form as by a written or printed statement, picture etc.

Copyright

Copyright is covered by the Copyright, Design and Patents Act 1988. However, with the proliferation and propagation of material via the Internet, copyright is a hot topic and the law will no doubt be reviewed in the years and months to come. The notes below are correct at the time of writing. Copyright is important for the PR practitioner, as there are many occasions when you may wish to or need to use materials created by third parties. It is advisable to get a lawyer onto the case if in any doubt about what is acceptable and what is not.

- **Copyright** is assigned to the author of the material, unless an employee in the course of working has created the work.

- **Copyright** expires 70 years after the author dies.

- **Assignment of copyright** is when the rights are sold to a third party.

- **Moral rights** give the author the right to be acknowledged and identified as the author when the work is used in any situation.

- **Permission to copy** written work must be obtained for:

    - extracts of more than 400 words in length

    - a series of extracts totalling 80 words or more

    - a series of extracts where a single extract is more than 300 words

    - an extract or series of extracts comprising more than 25% of the whole work.

- **Fair dealing** is the exception to permission to copy. Here acknowledgement is all that is required by the author. Fair dealing applies to extracts where the material used is not substantial, its use is educational or it is not being used for commercial gain.

- It is wise to include **credits**, acknowledging the inclusion of extracts from other author(s) works, in new works.

At present copyright covers:

- Original literary, dramatic, musical or artistic work

- Sound recordings, films, broadcasts or programmes

- Written and printed work

- CDs and recordings

- Video and audio tapes

- Photographs

- Pictures

- Drawings and illustrations

- Artworks.

Copying press cuttings

You need to obtain a licence from the Newspaper Licensing Authority if you wish to make photocopies of press materials, even for internal circulation. Contact them direct for the latest information and rates.

Passing off

> **Passing off** – the misuse of a brand or trade name of goods.

This is when one organisation wittingly or otherwise creates a brand which borrows a brand name, identity or design resulting in association or confusion with a competitor in the same trade area, which could damage trade or reputation. Companies accused of passing off have found themselves in long and expensive legal actions. Some companies, particularly those who are seeking headlines for obscure brands or who want to challenge a big brand in a 'David and Goliath' struggle, may feel it is a price worth paying for the potential column inches that may be generated.

Corporate social responsibility

Never before has there been such a focus on corporate ethics. Perhaps it began with the side effects of drugs, for example thalidomide and United Distillers. It has gained momentum with environmental issues and pollution, for example Esso and Exxon Valdis, and is now an issue for every organisation. We will deal with the management of corporate issues and potential crises in chapter eleven.

Long before an issue goes live or a crisis occurs, corporations should be thinking about their ethical stance. Cynics might say that this only occurs when precipitated by legislation, but more switched-on organisations know that early investigation, action and then consistent review puts them ahead of the game.

Works ethics committees or councils are becoming more and more common. Such a committee might consist of management and employees from all parts of the organisation, plus customers, suppliers and so on. Committees may also, and beneficially, include one or more independent lay-people, selected because they are:

- Expert witnesses, with an interest in the subject concerned

- Ordinary members of the public with 'man on the street's' concerns and views

- Authority figures – for example, academics or holders of public office

- Spiritual leaders – not only religious leaders but also humanists and philosophers.

Ethics committees' agenda and remit might include:

Environmental issues

How the organisation co-exists with and respects the wider world it occupies.

Investment issues

Whether the organisation's funds are used for good or ill.

Human rights issues

How the organisation deals with all the people and nations it trades/ works with, including distant third parties.

Animal rights issues

How the organisation relates to and the relationship it has with other sentient beings.

Patronage issues

Who and how the organisation relates to in terms of philanthropic connections or financial donations.

Checklist

✓ Familiarise yourself with the industry standards.

✓ Invest time in writing and agreeing contracts with suppliers and others with whom you have a commercial relationship.

✓ Refer to authorities for the latest position on issues surrounding copyright.

✓ Don't go in for slanging matches – unless you are 100% confident of your position.

✓ Always check current legislation.

✓ Audit your organisation from an ethical point of view – be ruthless.

✓ When in doubt, don't do it.

chapter five

Planning and evaluation for public relations

Introduction

Planning – five steps to success

Checklist

Introduction

In the past PR was highly subjective – what mattered was how you felt about a potential news story, how you judged a target audience might respond to a piece of literature, whether the MD liked – or didn't like – the media coverage you achieved last month. This was probably responsible for the negativity felt about PR by many business people, who believed that PR was a function that was difficult to measure, impossible to manage and undertaken by 'fluffy bunnies'.

All this has changed. Some of the change can be attributed to flatter management structures where everyone, including – and sometimes especially – the finance director, is expected to have an understanding of and views about the organisation's activities and whether or not they are making a contribution to the bottom line – because we are all now accountable. Accountability – not simply responsibility – has been one of the key drivers in the quest for practical and effective evaluation of PR effort.

But we ignore planning at our peril. Rigorous analysis and thorough planning is vital to the development of a public relations strategy that is seen to have worked. Time spent planning is time well spent and will make your work as a practitioner more focused, the results more effective and evaluation easier and more meaningful.

While in-house practitioners often assume sole responsibility for PR planning, there is a strong case for bringing in external consultants at the earliest possible stage. Planning developed as a specialised function in advertising agencies and has become one of the main services offered by major public relations consultancies. The objectivity from and range of resources offered by or through a consultancy can be invaluable in terms of asking the right questions, developing perceptions and gaining insight into the real communications issues faced by the organisation.

While evaluation is probably the principal way to demonstrate value for money and cost effectiveness, it is perhaps more importantly a dynamic way of delivering management information – and information, as we all know, is power.

Some organisations have more rigorous measurement and evaluation systems than others and this is particularly true when the expending of taxpayers money is involved. Other organisations simply want to satisfy their directors that the budgets allocated to public relations are achieving one or two very specific objectives. There will always be a handful of organisations where the man or woman at the top still judges the success of the PR effort in terms of the number of times his or her face stares out at us from the pages of the national press every day or how many times he or she is interviewed on the *Today* programme every month, regardless of any other PR effort or result. But it is increasingly true that growing numbers of organisations are recognising the importance of measurement and evaluation in PR planning. I believe that measurement and evaluation should be viewed as essential – if this is not built into your plan how will you know if you have succeeded or not?

Used at its worst, evaluation will help justify defensively what the organisation spends on PR expenditure. Used at its best it will encourage rational, analytical thinking that will enable the organisation to improve on past performance and achieve focused and defined results.

There has been more written about measurement and evaluation in public relations than any other aspect of the business over the past decade. *PR Week's* Proof Campaign, launched in 1998, has done a great deal to promote the understanding and practical application of research and evaluation techniques.

The IPR Toolkit researched and written by Michael Fairchild MIPR, first published in 1999, was revised and reprinted in 2001. It has probably become the most frequently cited text about evaluation and I make no apologies for referencing it extensively here. It is a practical workbook and provides examples and templates alongside numerous case histories. The new version identifies PRE (Planning, Research and Evaluation) as the three components to successful PR. I recommend that practitioners who are particularly interested in planning, research and evaluation should obtain a copy from the Institute of Public Relations (IPR) who sponsored its publication.

Planning

Devising a detailed scheme, method etc for attaining an objective

Evaluation

1. Ascertaining or setting the amount value

2. Judging or assessing the worth of

PR planning – Writing the PR brief

Rigorous self-analysis is the starting point. An understanding of where the organisation is now is essential for us to set a course to help us reach our desired destination. It's as simple as that. Spending time thinking is not a luxury – it is vital and will enable you to develop a brief which leads to a public relations strategy that is reasoned and logical.

You must be prepared to ask hard questions to flush out the important or hidden issues. This interrogation should give you all the information you need to write the PR brief. The PR brief is an essential piece of kit, whether you are going to use it internally, use it as the briefing document for a consultancy or write a brief for a client.

1. The marketplace

*   What market and sector is the organisation operating in?

*   What are the prevailing market dynamics? Any key issues?

*   Is the market growing or shrinking?

*   What are the current market/sector shares?

*   Which players are gaining/loosing ground…and why?

*   Who is winning the PR battle…and why?

*   Who are the main consumers/customers? Is this changing… and why?

2. The organisation

*   What is the recent/distant history of the organisation?

*   SWOT analysis – What are the Strengths, Weaknesses, Opportunities and Threats facing the organisation?

*   What is the organisation's culture?

- What are the overall:
  - Corporate aims
  - Strategic directions
  - Sales and marketing objectives
  - Existing/new products/services plans?

- How does the organisation see itself now?

- What vision does it have for itself in, say, the next five to ten years?

- What will help the organisation achieve its goals? What will stand in the way?

- Who are the key management players?

3. Public relations

- How has the organisation managed PR in the past?
  - In-house
  - Consultancy
  - Both

- What resources are allocated to PR? Is the person responsible for PR operating on his/her own on a day-to-day basis? How is the budget set?

- What skills does the current team have? Are there any gaps/needs for PR/general business training and development?

- Is there an international aspect to public relations management?
  - Central coordination
  - Local implementation

- Who manages PR in the organisation? Where does PR report to?

- What sorts of PR has the organisation undertaken? (corporate, consumer, B2B etc). What has worked?

- How is PR viewed in the organisation? What is its status? How does the rest of the organisation relate to the PR team?

- What is the internal relationship between PR and the other marketing disciplines? Advertising, sales promotion, direct marketing etc?

- How is media planned? Are there audits to ascertain the best media to meet the objectives?

4. Communications collateral

- What materials does the organisation currently have for the purposes of PR/communications?

    - Corporate ID and design 'guardianship'

    - Literature – consumer leaflets, corporate brochures, sales kits, branded materials, newsletters, bulletins, in-house and contract magazines

    - New media and AV – interactive website, CD-ROMs, video

    - Press kit – paper, folders, background releases

    - Branded merchandise – mouse mats, clothing, calendars, gifts, incentives etc.

- Who is responsible for this? Is it PR-led?

5. Research

- What research does the organisation have at its disposal?

    - Qualitative and quantitative

    - Continuous and ad hoc

    - Desk research

    - Media coverage analysis

If the PR brief is to be given to a consultancy as part of a pitch or tender process, then the following additional information should be included:

6. Consultancy pitch process

- What sort of response is required to the brief?

- What budget will be allocated to the consultancy?

- If 10% is allocated to evaluation, how will this be deployed?

- What is expected at the pitch itself?

- When will the pitch take place?

- Who will be working on the business?

Planning – five steps to success

The *IPR Toolkit* outlines five basic steps. In summary these are:

1. Audit – key questions

    Where are we now?

    What problems do we face?

    What opportunities are coming up?

    *   The audit stage determines current awareness and perceptions and defines issues – you should be looking at the organisation/product or service and their position in the marketplace as well as the target audience.

    *   Obviously the first time this is undertaken, benchmarking is a key issue, against which future activity can be measured.

    *   The PR brief should be constructed, setting out hypotheses. This brief should be refined through the period of the audit, assimilating research findings along the way.

    *   Some of this work may be undertaken by the PR practitioner (e.g. simple reviews of media coverage) while other aspects are probably best subcontracted to independent research specialists.

2. Setting the objectives – key questions

    Where do we need to be?

    Who are we trying to reach?

    By when do we want to achieve our objectives?

    *   SMART objectives are set.

    *   Stakeholders are prioritised and agreed.

    *   Budget is agreed.

    *   Timescales for the achievement of the plan are set.

3. Strategy and plan – key questions

How do we get there?

What do we want to say?

How are the messages best transmitted to the target audiences?

- Key messages are written and agreed.

- Training is given if required (e.g. media training).

- Tactics are selected and crafted – this is the creative bit.

4. Ongoing measurement – key questions

Are we getting there?

- Measurement of each tactic should be agreed.

- Data collection throughout the activity period.

- Specialist media evaluation analysis.

- Adjustment of plan if necessary.

5. Result and evaluation – key questions

How did we do?

- Analysis – lessons learnt, good and bad.

- Use findings to inform future planning.

Stage one – Audit

Data gathering techniques might include:

- Market research – qualitative and quantitative, continuous and ad hoc – these might include usage and awareness studies, focus groups, vox pops, telephone research, web research, postal questionnaires etc.

- Target audience analysis – commissioned or desk research taken from TGI, NOP, *Gallup* etc.

- Communications audits and attitude studies among stakeholders – internal and external

- Informal discussion – with trade associations, opinion formers, etc.

- Desk research – of reports and commentary on the market and the organisation e.g. Mintel, Datamonitor. The Internet is a terrific source of free and fast information

- Media analysis – using NRS, BARB, RAJAR etc and media packs

- Media audit – getting the views of the media on the industry, sector, issues and/or the organisation itself

- Review of media coverage – simple or complex depending on need and budget.

All or any combination of these data gathering techniques should be used at the outset of the programme, at regular intervals during the work, depending on budget availability, and at the end of the work to allow for evaluation. Planning is only as good as the quality and quantity of information that is put in. Don't make false economies by under-investing in information gathering. A properly researched plan will make the difference between wasting your budget on a campaign that fails to meet its objectives and one that hits its target.

Getting to know what you are 'PR-ing' – audit add-ons

- Arrange a trip round the factory, visit the head office and include a session in the Research and Development unit.

- Get a full product briefing, including a demonstration – use the product or service and get familiar with it.

- Get a briefing on planned new product launches, upgrades or relaunches.

- Look at competitor activity – work out their PR strategy and the messages they are putting out. Get onto their websites and look at their online press office materials.

- Understand the distribution channels – are sales direct or do they go via a wholesaler, dealer or distributor?

- Spend a day in a shop, behind the counter, on site, with the sales force – observe what is going on from all sides, as client and as customer.

Stage two – setting objectives

Objective setting

The objectives you set for PR should be SMART (**S**pecific, **M**easurable, **A**chievable, **R**esourced and **T**imed) and should build on the organisation's overall strategic direction and be synergistic with other business objectives.

Target audience

You may have a short list or a long list of targets which may include any from the following lists. Be focused in your selection and drill down to identify specific targets where you can achieve the most through more concentrated effort. Budget availability will also focus the mind in terms of agreeing priority audiences.

Internal audiences

Always include this important group in PR planning – they can be your most ardent, loyal supporters and ambassadors or your most cynical and jaded detractors – this group might include:

- Employees

- Management/directors/trustees

- Potential staff

- Supporters/members

- Unions

- Pensioners

- Suppliers (sometimes regarded as an internal audience by some organisations where they are working in close partnership)

- The media reaching these targets.

Get them on side and let them know what is going on. Where it is prudent to do so, encourage them to be media friendly, particularly if they might come into contact with the media themselves when out and about and give frontline employees media training if you know they could be targeted by the media. Work with your HR department.

External audiences

You will need to consider all possible external targets you are likely to have an interface and dialogue with – this group includes:

- Joe Public – broken down into broad groupings, which could include for example, consumers, women, parents, taxpayers etc.

- Professional groups e.g. teachers, bankers, farmers, small business owners etc.

- Opinion formers

- Pressure groups

- The local/regional community

- Government targets – MPs, special and all party committees, civil servants

- Customers

- Business partners

- International targets – for international programmes

- Financial targets – shareholders/owners, banks, financial advisers and agencies, the City

- Commercial targets – suppliers, wholesalers/retailers/dealers, customers, potential customers, competitors

- The media reaching these targets.

Timescale

PR is a continuous and sustained process and the programme should be structured over at least a one-year, but preferably a three-year period. Use planning aids for timing and build in contingency time for approvals, holidays and even seasonal and national events like Christmas and general elections.

Budget

PR is not 'free coverage' and you must allocate sufficient resources to do the job well. If you have a big job to do with PR, prioritise carefully during the planning process and tackle audiences in logical steps, one by one if needs be over the course of, say, three years. Don't try to do everything at once only to end up doing nothing particularly well. You will need to make budgetary allowances for:

- Human resources – you and your in-house team, your consultancy(ies) and freelance support when you need it (e.g. when short staffed, over peak periods and for maternity cover)

- Operationals – brought-in costs from third parties – including events management, photography, editorial promotions and expenses incurred in running them

- Administration – postage, fax, equipment, overheads – everything you need to keep the press office working on a day-to-day basis.

Key messages

These are the essential foundation for successful public relations:

- Define and agree your key messages so that they are understood by everyone who will be charged with delivering them to stakeholders

- Prioritise them so the most important is drummed home first, time and time again

- Keep them simple – don't use complicated language or jargon

- Go for messages which are motivating and memorable

- If you can par down your messages to a handful and really refine and hone them, all the better. Three is the magic number – more key messages than that and you start diluting their power and effect. You also make it much harder for your spokespeople to do their job effectively and confidently

- Start each with a keyword that summarises the message

- Give a little anecdote to illustrate each one.

When using the key messages well they enable you to structure what you want to say before you say it and help you stay focused, eliminating distraction.

Example

Three key messages for a 'beleaguered' retailer:

- **Customer-led** – everything we do, we do to meet the needs of our customers – e.g. our new wider organic range was launched in response to demands from our customers for everything from baked beans to olive paste.

- **Quality** – we will not cut corners or compromise on quality e.g. our in-store bakery uses only the highest quality white and brown flour from Canada which gives better tasting and better textured bread, even though it does cost a little more.

- **Staff-friendly** – our staff are our route to our customers and we know that the better they feel about working for us, the better the service to the customer e.g. our new staff uniforms are designed to be more comfortable and more fashionable.

Stage three – Strategy and plan

After assimilating all the research during the audit stage and agreeing defining objectives, targets, budgets, timescales and key messages, it is time to move onto the action stage.

Strategy is the overarching framework that defines how the PR programme will be executed. Strategies act as 'cement' for the tactical 'bricks'. It usually needs to be expressed in clear written format for wide communication purposes and may also be concentrated into a shorthand expression. For example the strategy for the beleaguered supermarket might be:

> *'Communicate that the organisation is 100% consumer focused, reaching business decisions based on asking consumers what they want, when they want it and how they want it, stocking products, brands and lines that people want to buy and offering a range of services and payment methods that reflect how people shop, served by staff who understand their needs.'*

A snappy shorthand expression might be:

'We put people first.'

The plan

The variety of tactics that make up the plan for public relations are discussed in more detail later in the guide. The list might include:

- Media relations

- Special events

- Editorial promotions

- Product launches

- Opinion leader communication

- Educational programmes

- Research

- Corporate ID

- Sponsorship

- Publications/literature/websites/AV

- Seminars, conferences and hospitality

- Visits and press trips.

Stage four – Ongoing measurement

You should measure public relations as you go and include observation and experience, feedback and analysis, and media monitoring. You need to monitor 'whether you are getting there'.

The way each tactic is to be measured should be agreed and data collected throughout the activity period. You might set up different criteria for each tactic, for example how many people attended a conference, how many visited the stand, how many came to the specially hosted event, how many leaflets or samples were distributed? If the date is collected in year one then a comparison can be made with years two and three to help work out whether this was a useful exercise. Research among delegates adds more important information and can be used to determine whether awareness, attitudes or behaviour are changing over time.

Media evaluation is becoming more and more sophisticated and new evaluation tools and software packages for measuring the quality and quantity of media coverage are being developed continuously. These packages also measure how consistently the key messages are being communicated.

Stage five – Results and evaluation

The key question is inevitably 'How did we do?'

Each year try to set out a measure of success against the set objectives. At the end of the campaign – say at year three – you can take a final measure and judge whether the campaign was a success or otherwise. If you have been evaluating at every step of the way you are more likely to have been modifying tactics as you go, thus increasing the likelihood of success.

Analyse what went right and what went wrong honestly and without retribution. Life is about learning – the person who never made a mistake never learnt anything. Learning the lessons, both good and bad from every PR programme you undertake, will help future planning and improve the contribution PR plays in building and maintaining your corporate reputation.

When reviewing consider using:

• Management reports – to demonstrate to your management team the value of public relations in the organisation

• Case histories – to tell the story of what the public relations programme accomplished, and why it worked in a graphic, narrative and engaging way

• Presentations – internal and/or external to show how the campaign worked for target audiences.

Checklist

✓ Obtain a copy of the *IPR Toolkit*.

✓ Plan over a sensible timescale.

✓ Get the facts before you start.

✓ Write a thorough brief and update it when new information comes along.

✓ Set SMART objectives.

✓ Prioritise if budgets are limited.

✓ Make sure the tactics are as creative as possible.

✓ Research and measure along the way.

✓ Evaluate at the end.

✓ Share results and lessons learnt with management.

✓ Use the lessons learnt to plan the next cycle.

chapter six

Public relations and the marketing mix

Introduction

The public relations practitioner usually reports either through the corporate route straight into the organisation's management team or through marketing. When reporting through marketing, public relations practice is associated with the marketing and sales process and so sits beside other marketing disciplines. But how does public relations relate to and fit with marketing, advertising and sales promotion? Should PR take the lead, rather than advertising, in determining strategy? Or is public relations really just media relations, just another technique, even an afterthought once the other parts of the marketing strategy are in place?

As a public relations practitioner I have been variously dismayed and delighted by the way other marketers have understood and interpreted the role and value of public relations within a marketing strategy. As a PR consultant, I have been introduced to clients by peers from other disciplines – particularly advertising and sales promotion – who have confidently announced that PR would deliver 'free space'. Likewise I have worked with PR people who think marketing is a dirty word. Turf wars can break out, usually if fees are at stake, and definitions suggest that there is an increasing grey area where anyone involved with the marketing effort could say 'hands off, that's my job'.

Public relations can play a fundamental part in the success of a coherent marketing strategy. Difficulties come from misconceptions and ignorance. Everyone involved in marketing should make an attempt to gain at least a basic understanding about the other's discipline so that synergy is achieved. If your marketing colleagues accept that public relations is about reputation, then pretty quickly they should arrive at the conclusion that it has wider scope than just achieving media coverage. The right public relations plan will deliver much more – it will help shift attitudes, surround your product or service with more positive values and imagery than the competition and thus contribute to the sales effort. Plus it will enhance your organisation's overall position in the marketplace. It may even have an effect on the share price.

When I worked in-house in a marketing team I was respected as a specialist in my field while still being an equal member of that team, which included advertising, sales promotion and direct marketing specialists. This is the position we should strive for if we find ourselves working inside the marketing environment. It's incumbent upon all of us as public relations practitioners to make sure public relations is recognised as being a central part of integrated marketing communications.

Consider a multi-discipline training course, such as the CAM (Communications, Advertising and Marketing) certificate, if you report through the marketing function. CAM students come from right across the spectrum of agency, client and supplier backgrounds. They work in marketing, advertising, public relations, the media, market research, sales promotion and direct marketing and are from both private and public sectors. So you get a good grounding, not just from studying with these people but networking with them too. CAM is also a nationally recognised qualification.

Definitions

Marketing

The management process responsible for identifying, anticipating and satisfying customer requirements profitably.

CHARTERED INSTITUTE OF MARKETING

Advertising

The means by which we make known what we have to sell or what we want to buy.

INSTITUTE OF PRACTITIONERS IN ADVERTISING

The promotion of a company's products or services to stimulate demand…

The use of paid-for space or time in publications, on the Internet, on television, radio and in the cinema, on poster hoarding's sites and other outdoor sites, as a means of persuading people to take a particular course of action or to reach a point of view.

THE DICTIONARY OF INTERNATIONAL BUSINESS TERMS

Sales promotion

Sales promotion comprises a range of tactical marketing techniques designed within a strategic marketing framework to add value to a product or service in order to achieve specific sales and marketing objectives.

INSTITUTE OF SALES PROMOTION

Direct marketing

Communications where data are used systematically to achieve quantifiable marketing objectives and where direct contact is made, or invited, between a company and its existing and potential customers.

DIRECT MARKETING ASSOCIATION

Sponsorship

The provision of financial, material support by a company for some independent activity not directly linked with the company's normal activity but support from which the sponsoring company seeks to benefit.

PUBLIC RELATIONS CONSULTANTS ASSOCIATION

The marketing mix

What exactly is the marketing mix? There are the much quoted 'P's of marketing – product, price, promotion, place, people, process and physical evidence. More useful is the list of twenty elements which the late Frank Jefkins identified. At each point, the PR practitioner can make a positive contribution which will enhance the programme.

Marketing element	PR aspects, issues, actions
1. New Product Development (NPD) – conception, innovation or modification of product	• Brainstorming. • Media monitoring of competitor activity. • What is the nature of the marketing opportunity? • Is the new product for established or new stakeholders? • Is it an unfamiliar product?
2. The place of the product in the product life cycle	• Is this a launch, relaunch, range extension, product reappraisal or revitalisation, managed decline or withdrawal? • The stage will determine PR objectives and strategy – e.g. to educate, to support sales strategy, to gain brand awareness, to reassure, to prompt a reassessment.
3. Market research	• Quantitative and qualitative research may form the basis for reports and interesting or quirky news stories.

Marketing element	PR aspects, issues, actions
4. Naming and branding	• A new name will invoke reactions from stakeholders – staff, customers etc. • Issues around a new name – memorability, distinctiveness, image, application – is this name close to another? • Will there be any controversy or offence? • Is it funny? • Is it a brand name that means something else in another language?
5. Product image	• Effect on corporate image or reputation? • Is it trusted? • Is it perceived as being high quality? • Is it a departure from the rest of the product portfolio?
6. Market segmentation	• Who is this product targeting? • Does this imply new targets for PR? • New consumers, distribution channels? • New media sectors?
7. Pricing	• Is the decision to put up the price, for example, going to have a knock-on effect in terms of sales volumes, company image or reputation? • Is the price so competitive that it will wipe out the competition?
8. Product mix, rationalisation and standardisation	• Will there be any issues with retailers and distributors? • Does a new product launch take the company into new market sectors? • Are there new media targets for this new sector?

Marketing element	PR aspects, issues, actions
9. Packaging	• Is it innovative? • Environmentally friendly? • Does it move away from a well-loved form? • Will everyone find it user-friendly? • Do retailers need to have it explained?
10. Distribution	• Who is responsible for distributing the product and what is the relationship like with these channels? • What is the educational need? Action might include: – Direct interface via facility visits, conferences, seminars, exhibitions, trade competitions, trade newsletter or magazine, training packages, trade press briefings.
11. Sales force/internal audiences	• Communications might include: – Intranet, conference, videos, CD-ROMs, cassettes, incentive schemes, reports, copies of press coverage, advance warning of marketing and promotional activity, house magazine or newsletter.
12. Market education, preparation or pre-selling	• Does the market need softening or warming up prior to launch? • Is there an issue our product or service will address that can be aired to get people thinking? • Communications might include: – Generic educational campaigns, literature production and distribution, press briefings, schools packs, specific stakeholder communications.

Marketing element	PR aspects, issues, actions
13. Corporate and financial relations	• How will this impact on corporate reputation and share price? • Communications might include: – Analysts' briefings, city page media briefings, bulletins.
14. Industrial relations	• How will this be perceived by the workforce and the trade unions? • Communications might include: – Union conveners' meetings, factory briefings, displays etc.
15. Test marketing	• How will the test market be conducted and who will know about it? • Communications might include: – Marketing press, local press, business press briefings.
16. Advertising	• Is the advertising highly original and creative? • Does it depart from past campaigns? • Is it direct response? • Is there a high spend? • Is it controversial in any way? • Does it involve celebrities or novel production techniques? • Communications might include: – Briefing marketing and advertising press, photocalls.
17. Advertising research	• Does it reveal any astounding new information? • Has the campaign been a fantastic success… or failure?

Marketing element	PR aspects, issues, actions
18. Sales promotion	• What techniques are being used? On-pack offers, BOGOF (buy one get one free), vouchers, competition? • Is this an entirely new promotion? • Are there any big prizes? • Who won? • Could the sales promotion go wrong/cause complaint? • Could the sales promotion breach any industry rules? • Communications might include: – Trade press media relations, announcement of winners to local press, issues management.
19. The aftermarket – after-sales service, spares, guarantees, instructions	• The corporate reputation could be severely damaged by poor aftercare. • Are there any issues which may emerge which relate to product quality or sales and service standards? • Communications might include: – Positive editorial features, satisfied customer endorsement and case histories, issues management.
20. Maintaining customer interest and loyalty	• Who has been wholly satisfied with the product or service? • Communications might include: – Editorial features, advertorials, testimonials and case histories, cultivating an 'ambassadors club' for advocates, loyalty schemes.

The decision making process

The decision making process – whereby a prospect becomes a customer – comprises five main stages, moving from awareness through to buying and then liking and remaining loyal to a company, product or service. Marketing and public relations have a role to play at each of these stages:

1. **Realisation** – where by the prospect recognises that he/she needs something. That something might be a face cream, a car or a pension. The need may be prompted because a previous item has gone past its sell by date or has run out – i.e. repeat or substitute purchase – or a new need is established. New needs may be prompted by editorial coverage, point of sale, advertising, sales promotion and so on.

2. **Information search** – whereby the prospect seeks information about what is available from manufacturers' literature, advertisements, editorial features, recommendations from trusted individuals (including journalists' reviews) or trawls his/her memory for stored information and past experience.

3. **Evaluation of alternatives** – whereby the prospect judges which is the best choice by evaluating information against a set of criteria which will include price, colour and other variables, brand name and values, availability and so on.

4. **Purchase** – whereby the prospect becomes a customer, convinced to buy as a result of successful marketing techniques.

5. **After-sales experience** – whereby the customer judges whether the decision to purchase was correct based on experience of using the product/service, its performance, possible loyalty schemes, the aftercare received from the company and so on.

Cause related marketing

Increasing numbers of commercial companies and good causes are recognising that, by teaming up for marketing purposes, they can work together for mutual benefit.

Objectives for the commercial company might be to:

- Increase awareness, raise the profile and enhance the image of the company, brand or service

- Increase goodwill and understanding

- Demonstrate social/ethical responsibility by associating the company with a relevant good cause

- Improve relationships with current customers

- Increase awareness among potential customers

- Gain competitive advantage/increase sales

- Boost employee morale.

Objectives for the good cause might be to:

- Gain stature by association with a well-known commercial company/brand

- Draw public attention to and increase awareness of the cause

- Raise funds.

The best cause related marketing campaigns engage with the consumer – according to research conducted by Business in the Community nearly 90% of consumers are more likely to purchase from a company associated with a good cause. Conversely people are inclined to stop dealing with a company if they disapprove of their business behaviour.

It is worth considering cause related marketing whether you are a commercial organisation or a good cause as the benefits can be considerable. With a strong supporting proactive public relations programme this sort of campaign can work very hard indeed. And don't forget to enter into a solid contract, even if you are dealing with a lovely, empathetic good cause. These days it's best business practice and an important management discipline.

Sponsorship

The objectives for sponsorship are virtually the same as those for cause related marketing. The main difference is that sponsorship normally relates to partnerships between a commercial company and another commercial enterprise:

- **Sports** – from the Premier League through to amateur swimming, there are phenomenal numbers of sporting sponsorship opportunities available to organisations

- **Arts** – opera, drama, jazz and pop concerts, art exhibitions

- **Broadcast** – sponsorships of one-off programmes, short run series, soap operas and even weather reports on TV and radio are available

- **Publications** – for example letters pages, special features and so on.

Sponsorship checklist

Key questions when assessing whether a sponsorship offers value for money:

- Does this sponsorship reach our target audience, fit with our planning and our objectives? (If not, stop right here!)

- Is this an entirely new project? Would we be the first to be associated with this activity? Who has gone before us and what benefits did they believe they derived from the sponsorship? What are the benchmarks?

- If an existing project, does this activity already get media coverage?

- How are the sponsor credits handled?

- What proportion of our target audience does this reach?

- What opportunities to see/hear are afforded? What is the cost per head?

- Are we one of a number of sponsors?

- What does it *really* cost? It's more than just the price of the sponsorship – it's also manpower, time, accommodation and travel expenses, hospitality, advertising and special packaging.

When budgeting for sponsorship don't forget all the extras including:

- Time costs – negotiation time, project management time

- Stand and display costs – design, build, erection, management and strike at every event

- Staff costs – salaries, temporary staff, uniform/costume, expenses, travel, accommodation and subsistence

- Product costs – samples, branded merchandise

- Promotion costs – TV/radio/press advertising, direct mail, posters

- Research costs – for post sponsorship evaluation.

Product placement campaigns

This is where a product is prominently located so it is seen and registered (sometimes almost subliminally) by the target audience. You might for example want to place your soap powder on the shelf of the corner shop in a well-known soap opera. You might alternatively want to prompt awareness of your new soft drink at a pop festival. Product placement is usually paid for and competitively negotiated. It is close to and usually involves some sort of sponsorship deal or reciprocal advertising.

Marketing through Channels

On many occasions organisations need the positive involvement of a third party – a wholesaler, distributor or dealer – who has a face-to-face relationship with the ultimate customer. On these occasions the PR practitioner may be able to bring new perspectives to the marketing planning so that all communications routes are explored, including e-communications, newsletters, media relations and so on. Additionally the PR practitioner may find him/herself getting involved with events, roadshows, conferences and seminars and may be responsible for the management and creative input.

Checklist

Use public relations as part of the marketing mix to:

✓ Enhance other marketing and promotional activity.

✓ Reach targets who may be difficult or uneconomic to reach via other techniques.

✓ Reach targets face-to-face via seminars, events, displays, awards schemes and ceremonies, demonstrations, presentations etc.

✓ Provide vehicles for more detailed messages or to present products in an unusual setting.

✓ Provide sampling and trial opportunities.

✓ Solve a particular short-term problem related to a product or service.

chapter seven

Tactics and techniques for public relations

Introduction

Media relations is, for most of us, the heart of the work we do and indeed for some practitioners – press officers, media relations executives and so on – it is the exclusive focus. Media relations therefore deserves separate consideration and is covered in detail in chapter eight.

But the most coherent and cohesive public relations programmes, underpinned by planning and a well thought through strategy, usually consist of a cocktail of activities to ensure that the stakeholder gets the message. And of course these activities can then become fuel for and support imaginative and effective media relations.

In this chapter we look at the tactics and techniques that the public relations practitioner may recommend for inclusion in a programme and at the pros and cons and some of the main logistical issues posed by each of them.

Face-to-face techniques

Seminars, meetings, exhibitions and conferences are a great way to reach your stakeholders in a very direct and impactful way. Thousands of events take place in this country every year designed to bring interested parties together, sometimes as a showcase for developments in a particular sector, sometimes for an overt sales purpose, sometimes as a forum for discussion of a major issue affecting an industry or sector. 'Virtual events' – for example satellite and online conferences – may contain an element of face-to-face contact by having live audiences in one or more locations, which are networked to the rest of the participants.

Pros

- Face-to-face communication is the most direct and, arguably, the most memorable and powerful method of reaching stakeholders.

- There is focus on the theme or issue – 'background noise' and day-to-day distractions are reduced.

- There is time for complex information to be presented and discussed in detail.

- Online and satellite links can network participants in any number of locations or countries.

- You can demonstrate corporate openness about a sensitive issue on a public platform (although this needs careful managing).

- Invitees can be made to feel special/important – 'this is just for me/us', 'my opinion matters'.

- If you 'own' the event (i.e. you are the organiser) you have ultimate control over the content, format and style.

- If you are taking part in an existing or new event organised by a third party, your organisation, product or service will be associated with the values of that event and the organiser.

- Smaller organisations may derive status by being associated with an event that puts them in front of a wider or more prestigious audience.

Cons

- You will have to work within or negotiate parameters set by third parties if you do not own the event.

- Unless you resort to online techniques, events require people to take time away from the workplace and/or home – not only those attending the event but also your own staff.

- The cost per head is usually higher than other PR tactics.

- You may have to hire and train external contractors to provide management and additional staff.

- There are often complex logistical issues to resolve – the bigger the event the more likely it is that you will need to think about subcontracting to a reputable event management specialist.

- You need to plan well in advance – sometimes a year or more – to secure speaker opportunities, the best stand positions, hotel accommodation etc.

You will find more on event management logistics in chapter fifteen.

Research

The use of research findings to generate media coverage is a well-known and – some might argue – even overused tactic in media relations. Every organisation – from the biggest government department to the smallest charitable body – uses research to give substance to and fuel their PR campaigns.

The research may be continuous research used by the organisation to show major, historical and comparative trends over several years, for example Walls's pocket money research and Farley's first time mothers' research. Alternatively it may be ad hoc research giving a snapshot in time or a piece of qualitative work looking at aspects of behavioural psychology among a target audience, for example men who buy red cars tend to be more outgoing than men who buy blue cars. Both continuous and ad hoc research can be used with a planned PR programme to help communicate the organisation's key messages and achieve its objectives.

Realistic expectations are key when considering research for marketing purposes. Many research projects launched to gain media coverage do not achieve their aims, largely because the research simply does not stand up as a news story and the media is wise to the use of research for marketing purposes. This is particularly true for the national broadsheets. However some are very successful, particularly when:

- There is a really good news story

- There are good case histories

- There is a sexy or quirky angle

- A strong supportive educational campaign is running alongside the research

- An A-list celebrity is fronting the campaign.

Some achieve excellent coverage in the local, regional or specialist press.

Research has many other uses other than simply generating media coverage – in fact you should consider how the research might be used in its widest sense at the early planning stages. It could be used to give the organisation a reason to talk to some key stakeholders in a direct and detailed way via, for example, the publication of a report or literature which is used as the basis for a speaker programme or conference work. It could be used to beef up an otherwise weak advertising or direct marketing campaign. On occasions, research has been conducted with one aim and that is to give the organisation some ammunition to go into one-to-one talks with opinion formers and influencers.

As always, the objectives must be agreed and the target audience(s) defined. A qualified market researcher should undertake research so that its integrity is unquestionable. The use of larger research companies such as MORI, NOP or *Gallup* can sometimes add value, as smaller or less well-known organisations can derive status and kudos from an association with a well-known 'expert'. Hiring a 'media psychologist' to act as a commentator and spokesperson is also now a well-used technique.

E-communications

An organisation's website is fast becoming the first port of call for any individual seeking information or any journalist wanting the latest news or background information. As such, your website must be considered as a vital component in the communication process, a resource for your stakeholders and a way of attracting people to your organisation. One word of warning – having a website is now a hygiene factor i.e. it's expected. So don't expect acres of media coverage if you are just about to launch a new website, are upgrading an existing website or have had a high number of visits to your website.

Whether you are responsible for the design and maintenance of your organisation's website or not, you should understand how it can enhance your public relations activities and use it proactively as a reputation management tool. As an absolute minimum, you should review the website regularly from the point of view of the media and make recommendations about its content. Every organisation should create and maintain a virtual press office online, accessed through the website. As basic background information you should include: annual reports, financial reports, a press release archive, product/service information, consumer research information, biographies of the most senior people, advertising campaigns and contact details. Online photo libraries are now a regular feature of online press offices. In terms of news content, be as up-to-date, as topical and even as controversial as you can be, particularly if you want to generate attention. Include news about people. Conduct and reveal results from research and surveys online. Work with partners and establish links with other relevant websites. Gather nominations and make awards online. Publicise events online, some organisations design exclusive online events and host live chat involving personalities. This can be particularly powerful for voluntary sector organisations.

Intranet and extranet systems allow you to get information out quickly and efficiently to your own staff or selected stakeholders who need the inside track. Discussion groups, that is newsgroups and mailing lists, which are used skilfully and subtly, can also enable you to establish communication channels with your target audience(s).

Online newsletters enable you to get to your stakeholders direct with editorial messages. There are many advantages to going online with newsletters – there are no print costs, paper isn't wasted, you can involve the reader by making the newsletter interactive and you can distribute the newsletter instantly to thousands of people. You don't need the newsletter to be the same length every time – online communications work better if they are shorter and to the point so endless thousands of filler words are unnecessary. Get a good and flexible design concept to work with. You can distribute the newsletter yourself – in which case you will need to create a subscriber list of e-mail addresses. Alternatively and particularly if you have an enormous list of subscribers you need to keep updated, you can use a company to distribute your newsletter for you.

You could upgrade and extend your online newsletter to become an e-zine. These are often web-based and so, rather than just text, use photography and video.

Pros

*   Window to the world – the website can be accessed by anyone anywhere in the world.

*   Intranets allow you to get to your own staff and provide a two-way communications channel.

*   Extranets can be set up which allow important named groups or individuals to access inside information not relevant to the general public – this has become an important communications channel to customers.

- You can update websites, intranets and extranets quickly and easily – vital for the dissemination of important information or in order to update status in the event of an issue developing or a crisis occurring.

- You can broadcast time-sensitive reports and results at the moment you need to.

- You can pre-empt bad news, deal with adverse commentary and issue rebuttals quickly.

- Extremely cost-effective way of reaching large numbers of people instantly.

Cons

- You need the resources to use e-communications well, principally people (either in-house or consultants) who know how it works and who are dedicated to maintaining the website, monitoring the Internet and analysing and responding to discussion groups.

- You need to tread carefully – for example organisations that are gung ho about using the Internet by overtly promoting their products and services, will turn people off. It's all about subtlety.

Multi-media

With the arrival of new and micro technology, there are lots of ways you can drive your messages home, engaging your target on a different level – to explain, educate or even inspire. These may be produced with just one specific target in mind – for example a business-to-business campaign might include a CD-ROM, a corporate campaign might include a video presentation, an internal programme might include cassettes. The tone can be authoritative, serious, rousing, and instructive or it can be just plain fun.

The important considerations are:

- What is it for? Materials may be required for one or more of the following purposes – company reports; internal communications and staff briefings; change management; education; health and safety; recruitment and induction; relocation or planning permission;

documentaries; business development; in-store demonstrations; corporate ID and design; visitors' welcome; media centre; issues management; post-crisis reassurance.

- The key messages we are trying to get across.

- Whether it is intended that the target should view material individually or as part of a group or audience.

- Where the material is likely to be viewed – at home, in the office, on a PC, on an exhibition stand, in a lecture theatre, on the move.

- How long should it be to do the job? The simplest rule is keep it short and sweet.

- Is there a need for more than one or multiple editions?

- What's the availability of the hardware needed to view the material?

Video pros

- Sound and vision – has the drama and impact of television.

- Useful as part of an event or briefing, especially to break up a string of speakers.

- Good for inspiring, summarising and demonstrating.

- Enables distant locations – which would be difficult and expensive to take people to – to be shown.

- Can be used to explain how a product works from the inside – for example how a new engine works or how a drug affects the human body.

- Footage has many applications within the marketing mix – e.g. on the website, media relations as video news releases, sales, marketing and advertising.

- Footage can be re-edited and new shots dropped in to update and refresh the presentation and keep it current.

- Cheap to produce in bulk.

Video cons

- Origination costs are high – don't forget music royalties and post production editing.

- Format may be selected by management for reasons of, dare I say it, plain vanity.

- Senior managers may not be good in front of the camera.

- You may need a professional presenter or celebrity involvement – this will add considerably to the cost.

- You may need animation sequences – which again will add to the cost.

- Special effects in post production ('morphing', combining live action and animation etc.) will also add to the final bill.

- Unless carefully planned or filmed in segments which can be replaced, video can look dated or become inaccurate quickly (e.g. showing old corporate ID or packaging, last year's CEO, old uniforms etc.).

CD-ROM pros

- Mainstream medium – benefits are broadly similar to video.

- Effective in reaching targets wedded to their PCs.

- Can include video footage of interviews with key people, case histories, presentations and materials that can be downloaded and printed etc.

- Cheap to produce bulk copies.

- Compact format makes it easy to post and carry.

CD-ROM cons

- Similar to video.

- Dependent on recipient's software and hardware, playback quality can vary.

DVDs will eventually replace video – and who knows what will come after that?

Developments in digital technology will have an impact on the selection of techniques and tactics used in public relations programmes.

The distribution and penetration of both software and hardware will determine if, when and which new formats are selected as the preferred medium.

Cassettes pros

- Useful in communications programmes targeting people who spend a lot of time in the car – for example social workers, midwives and sales people.

- Cheap to produce bulk copies.

Cassette cons

- Perhaps just a little old fashioned now?

House journals

These include company bulletins, newsletters, newspapers or magazines, produced for staff and/or external targets.

The main issue is – who is the reader? This will determine title, design, style and format, level of contentiousness, content, distribution, frequency of publication and medium (i.e. is this best produced as printed material or as an e-publication?). Potential readers might include:

- Internal – e.g. staff, management, sales force

- Distributors – e.g. retailers, dealers, wholesalers

- Current and potential consumers

- Patrons and supporters – e.g. donors, guests, passengers

- Opinion leaders – e.g. politicians, business leaders, academics, analysts, parents.

An organisation may decide it needs more than one publication. For example a charitable sector organisation responsible for a number of residential or nursing care homes may need:

- A weekly news-sheet for residents and their families

- A monthly newsletter for staff

- A quarterly newsletter for individual and corporate supporters and donors

- A quarterly magazine for medical researchers and specialists working in relevant fields

- An annual bulletin for local people whose homes are within a five-mile catchment area of all care homes (as supporters and volunteers).

It may be decided that because of the nature of the readership, all these items are best presented and distributed as printed materials rather than using electronic media.

One of the biggest mistakes organisations make is trying to speak to too many stakeholders in one publication. For example, a resident with learning difficulties in a care home needs quite different information and has very different needs from a consultant neurologist specialising in epilepsy.

In terms of customer journals, many retailers and service providers now produce excellent in-store and in-journey magazines which compete strongly with women's, home, general interest, travel and business publications. Produced for customers and frequently linked into loyalty schemes, these magazines influence other targets too and surround the retailer with style and panache. These magazines are produced by contract publishers with appointed editors and contain commissioned articles from leading journalists and top quality photography.

Literature and printed materials

There are many printed items which are used for communication purposes with specific target audiences. Sales literature may also form part of the remit of the public relations team. These items can be distributed reactively in response to general enquiries or can be used proactively as part of a direct mail operation, given away on stands, at exhibitions, roadshows and so on and to support media relations.

As always the decision to produce printed materials should be reached as a result of careful planning and examination of the organisation's objectives.

Literature might include:

- **Educational literature** – which explains the product or service or is related in a direct way. For example a leaflet on the health benefits of olive oil or how to cook using olive oil in place of butter for the consumer. There might be a need for a simple leaflet on the health benefits of olive oil for the consumer, explaining why high cholesterol is harmful, while a more detailed accompanying booklet for dieticians might summarise the most recent clinical research gathered from around the world with a digest of conclusions. The text of both of these could additionally be posted on an organisation's website with password access for the dietician. Educational literature might also include information packs and factsheets.

- **Corporate reports** – including annual reports, financial information etc. for opinion formers.

- **Research and other special reports** – which could for example summarise the latest developments in a particular market or explain the methodology and give the key findings of a piece of research. For example a study on the use of butter v. olive oil among families with young children across the UK might be produced to demonstrate why heart disease rates are likely to be higher in certain parts of the country in thirty years time. This might form the basis of a media relations programme and the report itself might be distributed to health visitors, doctors, dieticians and opinion formers.

Printed items might include:

- The organisation's history and mission

- Induction packs

- Staff handbooks

- Charts and posters

- Calendars and diaries

- Stickers and badges.

Copy, design, print and production of all these items are frequently the responsibility of the public relations practitioner and are included in the public relations budget. The public relations practitioner may even be charged with the task of acting as author and/or editor of copy but will usually subcontract to a designer and printer for the production of the piece. A working knowledge of the design and print process and the terminology used is important. While traditional printing processes are still used, we can expect a fast rate of change with the growing application of digital printing.

The design and print process in a nutshell

1. The brief

The brief is vital. It sets out what is required and is the precursor to the contract; it protects all parties in the event of dispute and clarifies the financial position. A brief must cover the following:

- Aims and objectives

- Background information

- Use of corporate ID, including colour and mandatory inclusions e.g. logos, addresses, credits etc.

- Target audiences

- Contact details – other parties who may be contacted for more information

- Format – i.e. anticipated page size and number of pages

- Style and tone – is it scientific, consumery, serious, amusing?

- Manuscript – what it will cover, the length and where the copy is coming from

- Illustrations – ideas about photography and illustration

- Print – paper quality, special finishes, quantity, delivery and distribution details.

- Budget – to include:
  - Copywriting
  - Design
  - Photography – original or library
  - Illustration
  - Typesetting and artwork
  - Print and origination
  - Delivery/distribution/mailing costs
- Timeline – when the work is needed with reasons for any urgency.

2. Copy

Either delivered on disk, CD or e-mailed document attachment.

3. Artwork scanning

4. Illustrations and photography

5. Roughs

These may be hand-drawn or produced using a Mac, with sample or dummy page layouts. This is the time to ask for alternative ideas and reworks if you don't like the roughs. Ask for a recommendation for typeface, unless corporate typeface is to be used.

6. Finished artworks

Once roughs have been approved, a final version of what the page will look like is produced. Starts to get expensive if changes are requested at this stage.

7. Final proofs

Typography and page layouts, illustrations in place. Check these carefully for errors and omissions.

8. Camera ready artwork

Ready to go to print – the 'point of no return'!

9. Colour separations

Production of printing plates.

10. Print and delivery

Producing literature – typical timeline

Week	
1	Agree objectives. Write brief
2	Brief copywriter/contributors and designer
3-4	Obtain estimates Prepare copy/content outline and roughs
4-5	Complete and circulate first draft copy for comment/approval Assemble visuals, photography etc.
5-7	Second draft copy Finalise visuals, photography etc.
7-9	Final approved text typeset. All artworks completed
8-10	Camera ready artwork to printers
9-12	Colour proofs from printers for final check. Print commences
10-14	Print delivered

Sponsored books

There may be occasions when a book might be considered to be an effective vehicle enabling an organisation to achieve its communications objectives. This might be, for example, when the organisation has reached a milestone or has been recognised as being the pre-eminent authority on an issue. While a book might be simply viewed as up scaled literature, there are some important differences and considerations:

- **Readership** – are we certain there is a market for and interest in such a book?

- **DIY or commercial publication** – the sponsored book division or commercial publisher will manage the entire process for you and give you important independent advice

- **Author/editor** – a member of the company or a commissioned and independent professional?

- **Contributors** – will they be approached by the author/editor or will the organisation contact and gain support?

- **Editorial policy, content and style** – will the organisation determine and control this or leave it to the discretion of the author/editor?

- **Budget** – is there potential for recovery of production costs through sales?

- **Shelf life** – how often will such a book require updating?

- **Distribution** – via bookshops or other routes?

- **Print run** – quantities required?

- **Promotion, merchandising and exploitation** – how can the book be used to maximise its PR potential? It is also worth bearing in mind that wholesalers and major booksellers will not stock a book unless they are assured that it will be supported with a substantial advertising or promotional budget

- **Evaluation** – qualitative measures via readership surveys, quantitative measures via sales and distribution data.

Design and corporate ID

This is a huge subject in its own right. There are a few points the public relations practitioner should bear in mind:

- The launch of a new corporate ID may be a wonderfully good or appallingly bad news story. When The Spastic Society metamorphosised into Scope with all the attendant corporate rebranding, it was both admired and praised. Arup's corporate redesign reflected its status as a drop-dead cool, world-class civil engineering company. But when British Airways dropped the union flag and adorned the tailfins of its fleet with ethnic graphics, the initiative was scorned and reviled. You will need to investigate the pros and cons from a PR point of view before deciding on the communications strategy.

- Any corporation must consistently apply its ID over all of the materials it produces, from its website to business cards, press releases to branded sweatshirts, literature to videos and on buildings and vehicles. Often the PR practitioner finds himself/herself as the guardian of the corporate identity.

- A corporate identity manual or at least simple guidelines need to be produced if many suppliers are responsible for producing branded materials.

Checklist

✓ Less is more – don't try to do too much, particularly if budgets are tight or if this is year one of a new planning cycle. Concentrate on doing a few things really well.

✓ Begin with the basics and build up to more sophisticated techniques.

✓ Select tactics based on what's right for your target audiences, determined through proper planning.

✓ Look at what your competitors are doing – and do it better or differently.

✓ Always include web-based tactics and make your website work as hard as it can.

✓ Get specialist help if you need to, especially if techniques are unfamiliar – use consultancies, agencies and freelancers.

chapter eight

Media relations

Introduction

For many people PR **is** media relations, pure and simple. And whether you're in-house or a consultant, media relations is probably the single most important aspect of the job for all of us, once the PR plan has been formulated.

In this chapter we look at best practice in media relations. Many books have been written on this subject – you'll find a list in the bibliography. I have taken into particular account the views and opinions of journalists themselves, and while it is true that they are often damning of PR people as a result of poor practice, they are equally glad to work with those of us who do get it right. Media relations is just a different game – you need to know the rules if you are going to become a good player.

What is 'the media'?

What media are we trying to have relations with? Simply any and every medium that is read, viewed by, or listened to, by our defined stakeholders. And while journalists and photographers and even TV crews en masse are frequently referred to as 'the press', each of the main media channels has unique characteristics.

Print media

Print has traditionally been the most prolific media. Be it daily and Sunday national broadsheet and tabloid newspapers, regional and local dailies and weeklies, general interest consumer magazines, specialist press for experts and enthusiasts, professional journals, business and corporate titles, there is a journal or magazine for everyone and everything.

The print media is particularly good for delivering detailed information, facts and educational messages. Readership profiles help us to identify the ones we need to prioritise and focus on and to address the greatest numbers of stakeholders.

Online media

With the rapidly increasing penetration of Internet ready home PCs, widespread web access in the workplace and the use of the web for adult education and recreation, the Internet is now used by everyone. Online media is now mainstream and effectively 'bridges' print and TV.

Newspapers now broadcast rolling news on the web 24 hours a day. What you see as a printed report is there as an electronic broadcast, accessible to a worldwide audience. E-zines are ephemeral and immediate and good for online demonstrations, immediate feedback, fast research and interactive involvement. This and the editorial environment allow you to demonstrate that you are at the cutting edge. Brand Republic (www.brandrepublic.com) is an excellent source of information and business intelligence from Haymarket Business Publications for PR professionals.

Broadcast media

Television

Television remains the most influential of all media in terms of delivering drama and communications via sight and sound to the mass market. The proliferation of specialist channels via satellite and cable has resulted in the ability to reach defined target groups, for example those interested in film, travel, history and children, the Asian community and so on.

Radio

Alongside the web and 24-hour TV news programmes, radio is the most immediate media with news being aired the moment it breaks, then on the hour every hour.

In addition, radio is a particularly effective medium for discussions and debates: for putting a client forward as a spokesperson or commentator.

News agencies

News agencies offer central and widespread dissemination of news and utilise electronic communication methods to reach international, national and regional news organisations. Larger organisations, particularly those needing fast information and access to news as it breaks, subscribe to these services. For some PR practitioners news agencies offer the potential for the most widespread dissemination of information.

Telling the right story to the right media
It is amazing just how often organisations try to sell a local story to the national press. This is so simple it seems almost daft to reiterate:

- Business/trade news – business/trade press

- Local news – local press and radio

- Regional news – regional press, TV, radio

- Consumer news – consumer press, TV, radio, online

- National news – national press, online media

- International news – online, international press, TV, radio.

Getting to grips with media relations

More and more PR practitioners are coming into the profession direct and so have never been journalists – and this is often a problem for journalists. The main complaints heard from journalists about PR people is that 'they just don't understand what my job is', 'they can't get the facts turned around in time' and 'they don't know the difference between news and corporate puffery'. We need to put ourselves in their shoes. We have to understand what journalists need and want from us in the same way that we have to get to grips with what we are trying to say about our organisation.

One of the basic issues is that there are several agendas at work. These are:

- The target audience's agenda – what's in it for me? Am I really interested in this? Do I need or want to know about this? (If I don't, I may stop buying this magazine/paper, switch channels or click to a different website)

- The journalist's agenda – is this relevant and will it therefore appeal to my readers/viewers/listeners? Is the feature right for our readers? If it's bad news, our readers/viewers/listeners have a right to know. If we don't get it right for our readers/viewers/listeners, we could lose circulation/ratings. Is this an exclusive that will help me build my own professional standing?

- Your organisation's agenda – how can we improve our awareness and favourability ratings through positive media coverage? How can we minimise and contain any negative media coverage?

In order to build relationships with the media we have to understand the journalists' agenda and work towards satisfying it and helping the journalists to achieve their objectives.

What is news?

The media is looking for news stories – not corporate information – and people in the media get mightily irritated by non-stories being flogged by PR people. The very first thing you need to develop is a real understanding of what is news – and what is not. You need to be sure that you have stories worth contacting the media about: otherwise it is a wasted effort. Ask yourself these five questions about each potential news story. The higher the score, the more likely it is you've got a fighting chance; the lower the score, the more you should consider a feature instead:

1. Is the story about important or interesting recent happenings?

   This means important and interesting to both the ultimate target audience and to the journalist. This is an important question because it helps to focus on both the stakeholders and the media most likely to be interested in the story, so you direct your effort where you are most likely to be successful. For example, the launch of a new beehive will be irresistible to the news editor of *Beekeepers Monthly* but may fall on stony ground if sent to the consumer editor of *The Times* – unless you know he is a keen amateur beekeeper or that honey will taste so different or the story is fantastically quirky. Also it's worth noting that, because of the way news travels in the electronic age, news is old very quickly. So assume recent means today and tomorrow but never yesterday.

2. Is the story about a subject or issue that is important to the general public?

   As a rule, the more people it affects, the more newsworthy a story is. Newspapers love a story where they can act as champions of the public, campaigning for the right to information and to publish material 'in the public interest'. The baby organ retention scandal at Alder Hey Hospital was major news because it involved thousands of babies and their parents and families. This helped to emphasise the national scale of the issue: one that potentially affected every bereaved family in the UK where a relative's body underwent post mortem. It was also of an issue every parent could relate to.

3. Is the story about important or interesting people?

Celebrities often attract media interest, especially if a photocall is offered. But real people, who have done something heroic or extra-ordinary, who have an important or interesting story to tell and who will take part in a photocall are just as good, in fact usually better.

Never assume that the media will find your chief executive interesting just because he thinks he is important. If he isn't inter-esting but dull, charmless or arrogant, don't use him as a media spokesperson. It's the organisation's reputation that is at stake and the spokesperson projects the values and character of the organ-isation. Get an outside consultant to help you deliver unpalatable truths to senior colleagues if you daren't risk your job.

4. Does the story contain information which is not already in the public domain?

This is the only exception to rule one. You may have information which is interesting and/or important, and involves real people but relates to something that may have happened some time ago. You may have the makings of a strong news story, providing it has never been aired in the past. This sort of news could however be viewed as a cover-up if there's a negative angle so be cautious and prepared.

5. Is this story something your organisation doesn't want printed/broadcast?

If so, then it's definitely 100% bona fide genuine news. The best news stories are laced with crisis, conflict and/or controversy. The good news is that most skilled practitioners – and the brightest and most responsible management teams – can turn a PR disaster into a positive opportunity if they act swiftly and deal honestly with the media. For more on this, turn to chapter ten.

The story, the whole story and nothing but the story. Questions the journalist will ask when analysing the potential news value of a story:

- Are things really as they seem?

- What's the conflict and who are the protagonists?

- Who are the winners and losers?

- Are there any skeletons in the cupboard?

- Is this a cover up?

- Is this just the beginning of a story that could run and run?

- Is there a political spin?

The news process

Once you are certain you have a story, you can consider how you maximise the chances of it achieving coverage. In terms of gathering news, the same basic three-stage process applies, regardless of media type:

Collection, selection, rejection

News intake is centralised on the news desk and the news editor takes an initial look at news just in. He/she will be using the 'is it news?' criteria to weed out non-news – so it's the first stage of selection.

He will then give a brief to the reporter, who will be asked to follow-up a story. The brief may be for him to follow-up a particular angle or to find more openings. Only the most senior correspondents have free rein. The vast majority work to a brief.

- With thousands of news releases being circulated everyday the competition for selection is intense. Virtually every organisation has wised up to the value of positive media coverage, from government departments and multinationals to small and medium-sized enterprises and local charities, and this has made the PR practitioner's job even more challenging.

- Hard news stories – a terrorist hit, a princess dying, a new treatment for cancer, the conviction of a serial killer, derailed commuter trains

– will bounce all but the most robust PR stories off the news pages. Even the tightest PR plan can't legislate for this. The lesson is don't simply target the news desks – get your story to the specialist correspondents and specialist media.

• It has been estimated that over 80% of media releases produced by PRs are binned. Many only receive a cursory glance, regardless of whether they are delivered as e-mails, faxes or through the post. Write well and only circulate newsworthy material.

• These days hard news is only delivered electronically – snail mail is now only really used for long lead-time media or when an item is enclosed which cannot be electronically transmitted.

When you have made a good contact in the media, then you can go direct to the journalist with a story. On these occasions you can choose to give an exclusive and may be able to offer an enticing one-off in-depth interview that will give the journalist the competitive edge. This may be an important and persuasive plus point when the editor weighs up the story's value during the selection/rejection process.

If you are not the source of the story, but it involves your sector in general or your organisation in particular, you may be contacted by the journalist and asked for a response. You may be prepared for this or it may hit you out of the blue. You may find yourself shifting into damage limitation mode using principles of issues or crisis management. The journalist may ask you to confirm or deny facts and is likely to seek direct quotes. Your organisation may be called upon to be an expert witness and journalists may come to you to obtain information they can't get elsewhere.

If on the other hand you have been proactive and put a story out which has elicited a reaction and pickup, then you should be prepared for any follow up that is required. Journalists tend to pursue a line of enquiry which reflects their own knowledge, feelings and emotions about the subject in question. Consequently journalists questioning styles vary enormously and they may ask superficial or very probing questions. Journalists generally don't want to haul you over the coals and the Jeremy Paxman/John Humphreys style is pretty much reserved for spokespeople representing organisations who are in the middle of a difficult situation.

In terms of making it through the selection stage, you will need to be fast and efficient and respect deadlines. You will also be expected to provide competent spokespeople and background information at the drop of a hat. Once the journalist has all his information, he'll write the story. He is likely to be under pressure and won't thank you if you fail to deliver on time, give incomplete or incorrect information or pester him for feedback.

The journalist never works alone. Once the story is written it will be passed to the news desk or news editor where it is edited for the first time. This might mean being binned in its entirety, rewritten by the editor, shortened or returned to the journalist for development or a rewrite.

Once the story is accepted, the 'subs' take over – their job is to ensure that the paper/bulletin goes out on time or that the website is updated regularly. They will also be responsible for ensuring that the house style is followed and that the news items fill the space available. At this stage the story may be shortened (or 'subbed'), photographs and other images (for example satirical cartoons) are added and accuracy is checked. The subs also write the headlines. The article may still carry the name of the journalist who originally wrote it (the 'by-line') but it may bear only a passing resemblance to the piece he submitted. It is unfair to blame a journalist if the story has been severely hacked about and appears to give a distorted view of the issue.

Selection and rejection are intertwined and there are hurdles all the way along the process.

Corporate expectations about media coverage need to be carefully managed – the organisation which expects lengthy news coverage of a new product may be sorely disappointed if a piece resulting from what was a lengthy interview with the Chief Executive is brief. But providing the main message is there and it is in the right media reaching the right target, you should count a news bulletin of even just a few lines as a success.

Building relationships with journalists

There is so much media that it's impossible to have good working relationships with absolutely everyone. These days it's quality not quantity
that counts. Journalists and media bods are frantically busy and, while
the offer of a slap-up lunch at the newest and hottest restaurant in town
may sound appealing, few people have the time to spare for a jolly with
a stranger if there is no real story in the offering. Lunch works best when
you have got to know someone a bit first and have the basis for a good
hour's chat with the passing across of decent material. And lunch is the
place for relaxed chat and industry gossip too. Start the ball rolling with
this suggested action plan:

- Identify the top five to ten media titles/stations/websites where you
  would like your organisation to achieve coverage – read them, watch
  them, listen to them

- Study the titles/stations/websites carefully and work out where your
  organisation could fit and where you might be able to tell your story

- Research names of journalists, presenters and researchers on key
  subject areas/programmes – aim for six to ten individuals in total.
  More gets unwieldy

- Approach these named individuals by offering an informal meeting
  over coffee/tea, or a drink, so that you can introduce your organisation. At the meeting hand over a short reference press pack with
  the website address. If they won't meet you for a meeting send
  them the press pack

- Try to make contact not less than once every three months. Invite
  them to informal events, one-to-one briefings etc. and feed them
  stories and feature ideas regularly

- Thank them if they write about your organisation favourably

- Don't harangue if they criticise but do take note and act on fair
  criticism

- Have lunch with them when you feel you have the makings of a
  relationship based on trust and respect.

Press conferences and press receptions

- Don't have a press conference unless the news is staggering or you are in the middle of issues or crisis management and the eyes of the media are on you.

- Work out how much it will cost per head either to hold a press conference or go out on a series of one-to-one briefings.

- Try out the idea of the conference – before committing yourself – with three or four journalists. If they aren't interested, don't go any further. You know you are onto a loser.

- Bill the event as a press reception, if you want it to be a lower key and informal occasion, largely held for networking purposes.

- If you do proceed, only invite the media likely to be interested.

- Choose a date that doesn't clash with another event, a competitors' event or a national occasion. Avoid school holidays if you are after consumer journalists, many of whom have children, unless you offer a crèche or entertainment for the children too.

- Make sure it's held at a time that will suit the majority of those you want to attend. Daily morning newspaper journalists often start work late in the morning (c.11.30am). Daily evening newspaper journalists finish work by 3.30-4.00pm. Avoid Wednesdays for weekly trade and local newspapers as this is often their press day. Sunday newspaper journalists usually don't work on Mondays and Tuesdays. Freelancers writing for long lead time magazines may need some quite heavy inducement to lure them away from their PCs and their studies in leafy Gloucestershire.

- If you are going for a press reception, these are usually held over breakfast, lunch, drinks or dinner and may feel much more like a party than a business event.

- Choose a venue that will suit the majority. Unusual venues may be beautifully creative but may be hopeless for access and travelling.

- The press conference is for the press – it is not a 'jolly' day out for management. Only have as many people as you need to do the job and give then all a specific role – no viewers, passengers or hangers-on – and never outnumber the journalists on the day.

- Call those invited the day before to confirm numbers.

- It is still usual to have a 'signing in' book on the press desk, although journalists and photographers sometimes manage to slip in without recording their presence, especially if it is a busy conference.

- Post materials on the online press office soon after the conference has taken place and send press kits by e-mail to those unable to attend.

Setting up a press office

Press offices come in all shapes and sizes. Some small organisations can manage perfectly well by allocating the press office function to a properly trained member of staff on a part-time basis. Others need a full-time, dedicated team of people working 24/7. In either situation the function may be subcontracted fully or in part to a PR consultancy. Form should follow function.

To help decide what sort of press office you need to set up, you need to ask yourself:

- Are you operating in a high interest/high issue or low interest/low issue sector? The more high interest/high issues you have, the more reactive resources you will have to allocate. And the more low interest/low issues you have, the harder you are going to have to work to gain media interest.

- Are you stimulating coverage with proactive initiatives or are you in mainly reactive mode? The more proactive you are, the more media interest you will generate.

- What are the aims and objectives for the press office and its press officers? The more aims and objectives, the more effort and people will be needed.

Press office checklist

- **Location**
  - Facilities and equipment
  - ISDN lines

- **People**
  - The scope of the role of the press officer(s)
  - Sector experience

- Consultancy/freelance support

- Admin/PA support

- Training needs

- **Resources**

  - Press materials – digital

  - Photo library – digital

  - Video footage – digital (digibeta)

  - Spokespeople – media training

  - Other collateral

  - Samples service

- **Communication and information**

  - Dissemination of information throughout the organisation

  - Journal reading and circulation

  - Press lists

  - Media monitoring (including online)

  - Coverage and circulation information

- **Budget**

  - Capital costs – kit and equipment

  - Running costs

  - Salaries/fee

  - Operationals – press events, reception, lunches etc

- **Evaluation of press office**

  - Media evaluation

- **Launching and marketing the press office**

  - Internally to colleagues

  - Externally to media

  - Externally to other third parties – partners, suppliers and customers.

Use a media contract log to record press office activity – you can circulate these contract sheets to interested parties.

Media contact log – checklist

Date of enquiry	
Journalist staff or freelancer	
Publication/programme and address	
Deadline	
Telephone number	
E-mail address	
Fax number	
Enquiry	
Information given	
Further contact required	
Issue date (if known)	
Name of person taking the call	

E-communications and media relations

- Agencies or news release companies now handle the mass distribution of releases via e-mail.

- Journalists go to websites first for background information on organisations, as well as to pick up the latest news and get the name of the PRO.

- You should monitor publications on the web, especially in terms of keeping up with breaking issues.

- Online information services feed journalists with the latest company news, background information, photography and video news releases 24-hours a day.

- Journalists are wedded to their PCs and are, like the rest of us, working under pressure – they are increasingly less likely to have the time to go out to meet people, attend press conferences or accept social invitations. Most prefer easy, fast, time-saving options – although a few still like a long boozy lunch!

Acting as media spokesperson

When working with the broadcast media, all the same rules apply. Additionally, you need trained, well-briefed and effective spokespeople who are able to represent the organisation and protect and build its corporate reputation.

Media training for spokespeople

Acting as a media spokesperson is completely different from any other sort of public speaking. It can be very daunting knowing that, while there may be just a camera operator and interviewer talking to you in the studio, millions of viewers may be watching you in the comfort of their living rooms. It can be very unnerving if you are expecting a confrontational interview or facing a difficult situation. The best media training makes you aware of what is going on, gives you an understanding about what the broadcaster expects, helps you prepare in advance and perform on the day. It is advisable to get your spokespeople trained and to use external specialists to help you if you can afford to. Working or experienced ex-journalists can help you get a real insight into what the media will want from you and how they are likely to behave.

Ten rules to help you write the perfect press release

1. Keep it short – try to keep it to one side of A4.

2. Present it for e-mail transmission.

3. Adopt a factual style – avoid corporate puff and over claiming.

4. Use clear layout – double-spacing and 'ends' at the conclusion of the release.

5. Tell the whole story in the first paragraph – who, what, when, where, why.

6. Use straightforward language and avoid jargon.

7. Include a quote.

8. Add a short pithy headline.

9. Include technical information and explanations as editor's notes.

10. Provide contact details.

Ten rules to help you write the perfect PR feature

1. Remind yourself of the readership of the publication and keep the reader in mind as you write.

2. Use language appropriate for the publication and the reader – this may include some jargon.

3. Structure it as you would an essay with a beginning, middle and end.

4. Open with a killer paragraph that attracts and keeps the readers' attention.

5. Provide illustrative support – photographs of the writer, product, people and places written about.

6. Use double spacing throughout.

7. Remain authoritative, objective and impartial – steer clear of corporate puff.

8. Write to length – sometimes a short feature will be 350-500 words while a longer feature may be 1,000-2,000 words.

9. Respect the deadline.

10. Be prepared for editorial corrections and/or feedback.

Ten rules to help you create good PR photography

1. Think images – you must be able to translate your story in to the visual media. People are the most important subjects in most instances. Go for close-in shots of people. Avoid groups of more than three people, unless there is potential for drama or graphic impact. Use celebrities carefully – they are expensive and can vamp your messages.

2. Work with a professional photographer who understands the way the media works – get the names of trusted photographers from publications. Some photographers help sell the picture into picture desks with or for you for an extra fee.

3. Write a good brief with the photographer.

4. Use digital photography – it is now the norm, it is versatile, compact, instantly transmittable and offers high quality. Digital photo libraries can be stored on CD-ROMs (forget the overloaded filing cabinet) and made available to the media via your online press office – you can embed captions – make sure and tell picture desks that there is no copyright on photos from your organisation (make sure you have cleared this beforehand). Photo-manipulation is also possible and adds all sorts of creative possibilities.

5. Set sensible budgets which include travel, accommodation, fee, props etc.

6. Try to make friends with picture editors on one or two of your key publications – trade press, regionals, local press and nationals if your organisation has the right profile.

7. Get picture ideas and photocall notices to photo desk diaries two weeks in advance.

8. Call picture desks before you send photos electronically – never send unsolicited material.

9. Contact the relevant journalist as well as the picture desk.

10. Think about timing carefully to increase your chances of coverage – for example get material to daily papers by midday for the following day.

Ten rules to help you get your story on the broadcast media

1. Listen to the radio, watch the TV and surf the web – get a feel for what makes it on air. There are many opportunities for PR on the broadcast media apart from news and features; the station's or programme's seasonal and thematic campaigns, for example on keeping warm in winter; general features; discussions, chat shows and phone-ins; promotions; sponsorships; what's on programmes; docu-soaps and reality programmes (but be careful of these as they are entertainment and your messages may be mangled!). As far as news is concerned there are obviously diary stories, scheduled weeks or months before alongside the breaking news stories. If there is one programme you judge to be the best to reach your target audience, make sure you listen to or watch most editions. Then when you do make contact you can do so confidently and knowledgeably.

2. Make sure the story you have to tell meets the 'is it news?' criteria and is highly people orientated. Research real life case histories and the human angle.

3. Watch your timing – regular programmes have weekly planning meetings. Consider long-term sell-in giving plenty of planning time and involving the programme.

4. Identify the right person to talk to – forward planning teams, producers, reporters, correspondents and intake.

5. Think about breaking news using news agencies – e.g. IRN, ITN, Reuters and APTN.

6. Always call before sending any material – then make sure you have a text to e-mail immediately.

7. Write specially crafted material for radio, TV and the web – standard press releases do not work well. Write crisp and colloquial material that reads well aloud. For TV write a **TV story advisory** which focuses on the visual elements and has all the elements that will make a story work. As a TV package – what footage is already available, filming opportunities, interviewees, press conference details and statistics/key facts.

8. Create pre-recorded digital video footage to broadcast quality – this may increase your chances of coverage.

9. Select spokespeople with care – make sure they are trained and have two or three main messages that they are comfortable and familiar with.

10. Be prepared to work unsociable hours to suit radio and TV production schedules – make sure your spokespeople are prepared to be flexible too.

Ten rules to help spokespeople appearing on radio and TV

1. There is only one rule – prepare and perform!

2. Check logistics and fellow speakers

    –   Where are you supposed to be and when?

    –   Transport – are they providing (they should do)?

    –   For TV – will they be providing make-up?

    –   Will it be live or recorded for later transmission? Live means that you have a good opportunity to get the messages across without later editing

    –   Who are you up against/with? Will they be hostile/on side?

    –   What is the composition of the studio audience if there is one? Pitch the message so they feel involved

    –   Check if any helpline number can be given – preferably given at the end of the show.

3. Get your three key messages clear in your head before you get to the studio – and make sure you get them in (in the most elegant way).

4. Check names of presenter(s) – don't get it wrong!

5. Dress comfortably but reasonably formally for television as you are representing your organisation

    –   Men – dark suit with a colourful tie

    –   Women – jacket with skirt or trousers (your bottom half isn't usually on display). Avoid black as it drains the colour from your face. Pastels are usually kinder. Avoid big jewellery – it Is distracting on screen

    –   Glasses – dispense with them if you can but not if doing so makes you squint or peer.

6. Communicate well and with energy and enthusiasm

    –   Remember to use language that people – both audience and viewer – will understand and never, ever use jargon

    –   Statistics can be very dull but if you have a really strong killer fact that enables you to 'paint a picture' – like 'one in ten men are suffering from impotence at any one time, an average of one player in every football team' then use it

    –   Use anecdotes to bring it alive – *'we recently worked with a company making oriental foods in Bath – we gave them advice and helped the company rethink their marketing strategy so that it is now exporting to over ten countries in the EU'* – it makes what you are saying all the more powerful and memorable.

7. Speak a little more slowly than usual – it helps convey authority. Also think about your breathing and try some simple breathing exercises if you're nervous.

8. Don't take any documents with you – rustling paper sounds dreadful in front of the microphone, is distracting in front of a camera and will certainly trip you up.

9. Forget the microphone or camera and try to keep the level conversational and lively, as if you were explaining your subject or point of view to a friend in the pub over a pint.

10. Finally, remember much of the magic is performance as broadcast media is largely entertainment – enjoy it, be enthusiastic and passionate about your subject and this will translate. If they like how you perform, producers and researchers may invite you back again and give you another chance to get your message across using these powerful media.

Checklist

Media relations checklist

 Do we know what is going on within the organisation to deliver a flow of news stories and features to the media?

 Do we have good news stories?
- New product
- New company – acquisition or merger
- New person
- New contract
- New investment
- New research

 Do we have good features?
- Expanding a news story
- Review of organisation's products and/or services
- Interview with or think piece from organisation's figurehead
- Market/sector analysis or developments in the sector
- Educational backgrounder
- Tried and tested feature
- Regular columns e.g. advice and letters columns

 Is the media material well written?

 Is the media tailored for different media sectors and target audiences?

✓ Are our media lists up-to-date?

✓ Which named media could we deliver this story to in advance, to stimulate quality media coverage?

✓ What is the best route(s) out to the media?

    – One-to-one briefings with key media

    – E-release and posted on the website

    – Press release via mail

    – Press conference/online press conference/press reception

✓ Do we have good images?

    – Digital pictures

    – Portraits of key personnel and spokespeople

    – Captions

✓ Do we have enough samples/literature for media distribution?

✓ Are the spokespeople fully briefed and media trained?

✓ When should the story be released?

    – Share price and other corporate sensitivities/regulatory issues

    – Distribution in place

    – Spokespeople available

✓ Is the press office staffed/switchboard briefed?

✓ Who will manage media relations out-of-hours and are contact details up-to-date?

✓ Is there a need for other briefings?

    – Internal

    – Suppliers

    – Distributors/dealers

    – Customers

    – Opinion formers

chapter nine

Managing public relations

Introduction

For some organisations, PR is a management function, a central part of the organisation's continuous communications process with all its target audiences. For others PR is positioned as part of the marketing support function. Regardless of its place in an organisation, PR needs to be managed like any other business activity, and this includes analysis of your organisation's PR needs, objective setting, programme planning, consulting, resourcing, budgeting, implementation, reporting and contingency planning.

We have looked at analysis and planning elsewhere in this guide. So here we will concentrate on some of the most important practical management issues facing the public relations practitioner, including using a PR consultancy.

Budgeting

I have heard of some strange ways of working out a budget for public relations over the years. For example, one organisation used a rule of thumb that said a third of the budget should be spent on fees and two-thirds on bought-in costs – completely off the mark given that the programme was issues and crisis management orientated. Another organisation planned on allocating one tenth of the overall marketing budget to public relations, a half on advertising and the rest on sales promotion.

The plain truth is that you budget either 'top down' or 'bottom up':

*   The optimum PR plan is written and is designed to achieve all set objectives and reach all target audiences. A budget is then allocated to cover all aspects.

*   A finite budget is set and a PR plan is constructed using available resources. The emphasis may be one or two priority stakeholders groups and objectives.

It's a simple as that.

You should also have a benchmark of what has been spent on public relations in the past – unless this is a first time process.

There are four main costs:

- Human resources – salaries and/or consultancy fees

- Operationals – from sandwiches for working meetings through to venue hire and advertorial costs

- Administration – what it costs to run the operation from telephones and stamps, to light and electricity

- Planning, research and evaluation – so that you can learn from what you do for future planning purposes.

Managing the in-house function and in-house teams

Having worked in-house myself and also having worked alongside many clients' in-house teams I would suggest that there are three main issues in-house practitioners need to address:

Perception

What do your colleagues understand about or think about PR? Are perceptions favourable or unfavourable? Are people willing to work with you? Are you getting the right feed of information? You may need to do an internal PR job to improve matters or to make sure colleagues have a better understanding of the role of PR within the organisation.

Status

What is the position of PR in the organisation? Is PR seen to be at the heart of the organisation's communication strategy or simply as an adjunct to marketing? Again you may have to do quite a lot of work to improve the situation.

Isolation

If you are the only PR practitioner in the organisation or have a very small team I feel it is vital to get involved with external professional PR people and to network. Get out to industry events, join the Institute of Public Relations, get yourself a mentor or at least a peer buddy from another organisation, create an informal group of other PR people drawn from the industry you work in or the town your organisation is based in. I heard of a group of PR people working for companies on a large industrial estate who organised bi-monthly get-togethers at the local pub.

They helped sort out each other's problems, passed on ideas and information about local media and were a great supportive network.

Leading a PR team is just the same as any other sort of team management in terms of developing leadership skills, particularly if you are managing graduates with no experience who need skills training and on the job coaching.

In-house consultancy

At some point, most organisations need to weigh up the pros and cons of managing their public relations entirely in-house or by subcontracting part or all of the work to a consultancy.

Pros	Cons
In-house PR	**In-house PR**
• Familiar with own organisation	• You may have to start up a department from scratch – recruitment and resourcing costs may be considerable
• In-house PR is usually a full-time post	
• Can establish lines of communication internally more quickly by being on site	• Could be so enthusiastic about the organisation or subject or so close to the issues that he/she is unable to see the 'wood for the trees' and fails to be objective
• Onsite means on the spot:	
– To deal with issues or crises	
– To get consensus/ decision quickly	• May be isolated – the only person responsible for PR in the organisation
– To give day-to-day and immediate advice to management and others	• May spend time not doing PR, sidetracked to other functions especially in marketing departments
• In-house practitioners are better placed to identify potential news stories, promotional opportunities and potential issues	• Job title can be open to interpretation and may not reflect what job is actually about (e.g. publicity executive, marketing executive etc.)
• If properly positioned he/she may achieve status as an internal consultant	
• Journalists may prefer to phone an in-house practitioner – providing he or she is reliable and delivers	• May be used as a political football for rival individuals or departments who are, for example, competing for profile

Pros	Cons
• May have excellent media contacts in trade and business press	• May not have executive status, so ability to influence corporate strategy may be limited
• The in-house practitioner may have or acquire specialist knowledge of the sector or subject	
• Can brief out and manage contracts or projects to consultancies or freelancers	

Consultancy	**Consultancy**
• Independent – able to be objective and offer impartial analysis and advice	• Remote – may find it difficult to access the right people quickly
• Consultancy team can be tailored to include different calibre staff to suit client brief	• May find it time consuming to develop an in-depth under-standing of operational issues
• Can perhaps challenge senior people more easily than the in-house practitioner	• Access into the client may be through just one person
• Specialist practitioner – all the consultant does is PR	• PR programme is limited by the size of the fee paid to the consultancy
• Experience is gained with many clients working to different strategies and using diverse techniques	• Possibly distanced from decision-making at higher levels within the client organisation
• May have strong media contacts as a result of working on a number of clients in the same sector	
• Can access other members of the consultancy team for brainstorming, a second opinion etc.	
• If full service or part of a group may also have access to specialist services and facilities	
• Staff costs (NI, sick pay etc.) are borne by the consultancy	

What do PR consultancies offer?

You can subcontract to full service and/or specialist consultancies. Full service will offer many of the following while specialists will give you exclusive focus on one specific area:

- Media relations;

- Marketing communications;

- Public affairs;

- Corporate communications;

- Business-to-business programmes;

- Financial PR;

- Internal communications;

- Community relations programmes;

- International PR;

- Issues and crisis management;

- Healthcare PR;

- Consumer PR;

- Sponsorship;

- Cause related marketing;

- Ethical auditing.

Once the decision has been made to call on an external consultancy, you will need to work through the pitch process.

The pitch process

Question 1

Why do we need a PR consultancy?

Answer(s)	Comments
• Objectivity	Should give independent and objective consultancy advice.
• Strategic skill	Intellectual strength and application.
• 'Another pair of hands'	Maybe you just don't have enough resources in-house.
• Specialist experience	Important if you are moving into a new market or targeting a new audience.
• Good media contacts	Which should complement your own contacts.
• Added skills	Which you don't have, like event management or public affairs.
• Creativity	Always important in a competitive marketplace and if you are seeking a greater share of voice.

Question 2

We already have consultancy support – what do we do?

Answer(s)	Comments
• Account review	To ensure everyone is on track, client/consultancy relationship remains positive, programmes are refreshed and results are consistently maintained/exceeded, it's a good idea to have a formal annual review and to involve everyone who has a relationship with the consultancy.
• Account repitch	To give the incumbent and others the chance to pitch for a bigger, different or additional contract with new requirements – you must be committed to and prepared to switch consultancies if a new consultancy's response is more appropriate, inspired, insightful or gives better value for money. Pitches cost consultancies a great deal in terms of time and effort so only do this if all invited to pitch, including the incumbent, have an equal chance of winning.
• Contract termination	The last resort if the consultancy can no longer service the account or answer the brief, the relationship has collapsed, strategy has been weak, budget management has been poor or results have been mediocre – before you take this radical step make sure you understand how responsible your organisation has been for getting to this stage, acknowledge this and learn from your own mistakes too.

Question 3

What sort of consultancy do we need?

Answer(s)	Comments
• Specialist practice	With expertise and a track record in your industry or sector for targeting the stakeholders you want to reach.
• Full service – public relations/public affairs/event management	Where a fully coordinated and synergistic approach is needed.
• Local/national/ international capabilities	Are you planning a centralised strategy rolled out across regions and countries? Do you want coordination or implementation?
• Part of group offering other marketing services – advertising, direct marketing, sales promotion	You may need or prefer a one stop shop for a coordinated marketing communications campaign.

Question 4

How do we get to a 'long list'?

Answer(s)	Comments

• Consult:
  – PR Register
  – PRCA
  – *PR Week* league tables and reports
  – Hollis press and PR annual
  – Other directories
  – Trade associations
  – Websites
	PR Register and PRCA both provide a search service for clients, for a fee of course!
	
	Industry media is always useful for ideas and for news about consultancies and who is hot and who is not.

- Ask:
  - Journalists
  - Competitors
  - Suppliers e.g. your advertising agency
  - Colleagues

Most individuals – especially journalists – will give you an honest assessment of who they think does the job well.

- Review the organisation's past use of consultancies

Learn from past experience but remember times change, businesses develop and people move on – a consultancy your organisation sacked ten years ago is likely to have reinvented itself over the intervening period. Don't rule out good candidates for the wrong reasons.

- Make a long list of five to six consultancies – look at websites

Don't be seduced into looking at more – and make it less if at all possible. It's simply a waste of everyone's time.

- Subcontract to a specialist company

There are a number of management consultancies who will manage the process for you if you need this support.

Question 5

How do I manage the selection process?

Answer(s)

Comments

- Write the first draft of the brief with colleagues' input

Make sure everyone who will be involved in the decision making process has a chance to input to or review the brief.

- Make contact

Talk to the consultancies – you will probably be referred to the New business/Business development director in the first instance (this person probably won't work on your account but may be part of the pitch team if they get over the first hurdle).

- Select short list for credentials pitch – three to four consultancies

Tell the others promptly that they haven't gone on to the next stage – tell them why so they can learn from this. Ask for part of the credentials pitch to concentrate on fees, budgeting and ethos. Ask for the people who might work on your account to be present – this will help you think about chemistry and fit. Work out a scoring or assessment system for those responsible for judging the pitches so common criteria are used (see below for a suggested checklist). Again stay focused and arrive at a final short list of two to three – don't try to do more unless it is absolutely impossible to make a decision.

Question 6

How do we run the pitch?

Answer(s)	Comments
• Inform the contenders	And again let those not selected to go on to the next stage know promptly – give reasons if you can. Some clients let the short listed consultancies know who they are up against – this seems to me to be fair and grown up in the age of transparency and accountability.
• Finalise and give the brief	See the chapter on planning to help determine what needs to go into the brief. Make sure all contenders have the same brief and that they are clear on the decision making process.
	Try to give a realistic idea about the budget – you may think that, by not giving a budget, the consultancy will be more motivated or will be more creative – or you might think that if you are up front about the budget they will either decline to pitch or will assume the sky is the limit. But you won't be judging like with like if everyone works on blue sky budgets and, more importantly, while you might get fabulous, wacky all singing all dancing creative ideas, you won't get a feel for what is realistically achievable unless you give a realistic, honest ballpark figure.
	Allow time for meetings and questions before the pitch, including facility visits and give all contenders the same degree of access.
	Give a critical path and ask for a written submission in advance of the presentation so you can do justice to any detailed strategic thinking or research the consultancy may have undertaken.
	Make sure everyone who will be responsible for the decision making is available and booked for all pitches.
	If you are seeing two or three consultancies try to see them on the same day; if more, keep the presentation times as close together as possible.

Question 7

So how do we decide?

Answer(s)	Comments
• Use common criteria	If all the decision makers have used a set of common criteria then you can compare like with like and will be able to debate specific ideas.
• Have 'get real' meetings	Get together after the pitch to thrash out any details that aren't crystal clear – like budgets and fee charging – and to meet the actual team if they weren't present at the pitch.
	Get references from other clients; call them and ask them what it is like to be this consultancy's client, warts and all.
• Decision time – making the appointment	Write to everyone to let them know your decision one way or the other and give reasons so they can learn from the experience.
	Work together on a press release to announce the appointment.
	Get a formal contract in place as soon as possible.
	Agree schedules of monthly and quarterly meetings and fix the date for the annual review.

Pitch assessment criteria – sample template

Name of company _____

Please allocate a mark out of ten for the quality of the presentation in addressing each of the following criteria.

Criteria	Comment	Score
Overall understanding of our organisation and the issues and challenges facing us.		
How accurate is their understanding and assessment of our target audiences?		
How compatible are their creative ideas with our existing corporate or brand values?		
How do you rate the impact of their creative ideas?		
How do you rate their strategic recommendations?		
How do you rate their advice regarding timing of suggested campaigns?		
How do you rate the company's professionalism and ability to deliver?		
How do you rate the company's ability to evaluate the effectiveness of the campaign?		
How do you rate the company's experience of undertaking other relevant campaigns?		
Overall, the extent to which you feel the company should be appointed?		
	Total score	

Suggested shortlist criteria

- Does the consultancy have the right experience, expertise and facilities?

- Who are the current clients? What is the rate of client retention/churn? How long on average do clients remain with the consultancy?

- Are there any client conflicts? (i.e. does the consultancy already work with clients who we already work with or might compete with?)

- Did we see any relevant case histories? Were the results positive?

- Does the consultancy have a good reputation?

- How long has the consultancy been in business?

- Could we get on with the team on a personal as well as professional basis?

Checklist

✓ Negotiate a realistic PR budget that enables you to achieve your objectives.

✓ Make sure you have enough in-house resources to either manage the PR internally or manage a consultancy or consultancies.

✓ Get your team trained effectively – if they are to be responsible for consultancy management give them specific training to make sure they do this professionally.

✓ Market the PR team/department and its work and achievements internally.

✓ Decide whether you need external consultancy or freelance support.

✓ Work through the pitch process methodically.

✓ If you are a consultant, understand the pitch process and help clients with it.

chapter ten

Issues and crisis management

Introduction

Corporate and financial public relations has been a great success. We – and the media – are now interested in organisations, in the rises and falls, the successes and failures, the good guys and the bad guys. Organisations make news and the best news has some element of controversy or conflict, tension and human interest, intrigue and cover up. Given that corporate ethics and responsibility are now widely discussed organisations need to get it right and behave themselves or there will be trouble ahead. The media spotlight is on organisations, whatever the sector, whatever the business. So the organisation that finds itself in difficulties, commits real or perceived misdemeanours or causes harm to human life, animal life or the environment is certain to make the headlines.

Some organisations call in the media team when the issue is about to break or when the crisis has taken place. This is just too late. The definition of public relations talks about a planned and consistent approach and this is just what issues and crisis management is all about – preparation before the event and performance when it – whatever *it* is – happens. No organisation can afford to ignore this planning. The reputation which you have worked so hard to build and nurture should be protected in the event of the unexpected.

You will need to be scrupulous about your preparation and interrogate both the broad issues facing your sector or industry in general and then the particular issues facing your organisation.

- What are the worst things that could happen as a result of your corporate activities?

- How would your organisation respond?

When an issue breaks or a crisis occurs, do not ignore your own responses which may include:

- **Physical effects** – raised heart rate, sickness, the shakes, fight and flight

- **Psychological effects** – anxiety, fear, anger, guilt, sadness, paralysis

You will be under particular stress – issues and crisis management is a 24/7 job and you'll need to be ready for every eventuality. Good planning for issues and crisis management will help you take action even if you feel paralysed by the events which may overtake you.

If your organisation faces an issue or crisis, friends may desert you if you fail to communicate properly as they may feel they will be embroiled in your problems. Foes may use the opportunity to gain a competitive advantage or even put the boot in. They will give their version of the story if you don't talk to the media and you can be certain they won't do you any favours. Don't go underground and never, ever say 'no comment'. You are abdicating your corporate responsibility.

Organisations facing an issue or crisis tend to behave in one of two ways – they either take a negative approach (we have something we must minimise/ignore/cover up because it will threaten our reputation – let's say nothing) or they see the positive side (we must face up to this and be proactive as this will help to rebuild/enhance our reputation – let's tell people what's happened and what we are doing).

You need the buy-in of your top management in issue and crisis planning. When the going gets tough and corporate reputation is at stake, the senior team will need to get involved and lead by example, demonstrating that they are taking this seriously. The reputation of the organisation is ultimately their responsibility.

The purpose of this chapter is to help you think now so that you can act positively when you need to. We will look at the preparatory stages necessary for good issues and crisis management and then the main practical issues and the immediate action that is needed. The good news is that it is all common sense, tempered with a liberal dose of pragmatism and humility and a strong willingness and ability to communicate.

Definitions

Is it an issue – or is it a crisis?

Dictionary definitions imply an issue is less dramatic than a crisis – the difference is rather like that between a chronic illness – which goes on for a long time – and an acute condition – with a rapid onset and potentially equally rapid conclusion.

'**issue** – *a topic of interest or discussion – an important subject requiring a decision – (legal) the matter remaining in dispute between the parties to an action after pleading*'

'**crisis** – *a crucial event or turning point – an unstable period especially one of extreme trouble or danger – a sudden change in the course of a disease*'

Many public relations practitioners have offered other definitions:

'**issue** – *unexpected bad publicity*'

'**crisis** – *an issue in a hurry*'

'**crisis** – *a serious incident which has or will affect human safety, or is threatening to life and/or health and/or the environment*'

The newspaper magnate William Randolph Hurst said that '*news is whatever someone, somewhere does not want published*'.

The fact is that a major issue can be at least as damaging to an organisation as a crisis. If we ignore this fact we ignore a great truth – that the professional and effective daily handling of an issue, sometimes over months and years, is as critical as the immediate handling of a dramatic incident.

I would offer the following definition which attempts to capture the close relationship between an issue and a crisis for the public relations practitioner:

'*A sudden incident or a long-term problem – possibly triggered by a sudden incident – which could damage an organisation's reputation, affect its share price and impact upon the way it is able to conduct itself in the future.*'

Issues and crisis audit

The first step is a thorough audit of the organisation's interests and activities to flush out risk areas and vulnerabilities. You can call in specialist risk managers to help with this process if your organisation is particularly large or complex. Risk managers seem to be particularly good at defining the potential financial impact that loss of reputation might have on your organisation or brand – and this seems to help focus corporate minds on the subject!

Some organisations have an ethics panel or ethical review process. This may be a good forum to tap and a fertile place to harvest ideas about issues your organisation may be facing.

Use the following list of questions to get you started – and brainstorm others. You must be completely honest – it's usually the issue that has been swept under the carpet that proves to be the most problematic.

What are the main industry/sector issues? (e.g. health and safety, 'excessive' profitability, exploitation etc.)

Are there any legislative issues which could have an impact on our ability to conduct our affairs? (e.g. tax measures, employment law etc.)

Are there any global issues which could have an impact on the way we conduct our affairs? (e.g. commodity prices, war zones, sanctions etc.)

Is there any area of our operations which could give campaigners cause for concern on any level? Is our industry, sector or organisation being targeted by pressure groups? (e.g. ethical, environmental, human rights, animal rights, religious groups etc.)

Are there any issues relating to the integrity or good character of our management team/staff/consultants/suppliers/past employees?

Are there any issues regarding our premises or sites? (e.g. health and safety, security, upkeep, locality etc.)

Are there any issues regarding the quality of our work/products/services? (e.g. repeat customer complaints, product failure, withdrawal etc.)

Have we ever had an issue in this organisation in the past? How did we handle it? Has the problem been resolved? Could it recur?

Once you have honestly faced up to the issues within your sector and your organisation, you can start thinking about your strategy. If it is a problem that concerns only your organisation, then do something about it immediately. If you can't solve the problem immediately then prepare a plan for doing so with timescales and responsibilities clearly outlined.

Issues management

An issue is an issue is an issue – some hit the headlines and then go on to be news for months and even years. Think of food safety and BSE, rail safety and Ladbroke Grove, drug side effects and thalidomide, animal experimentation and Hillgrove, intensive farming and foot and mouth. The issue flares again as a news story with the release of new research, another similar case, a case history, a story on the Internet or a related overseas incident.

This poses problems for the public relations practitioner and for the management of the public relations process. With news flowing across the Internet as soon as it happens, you must accept that you will not always be in control. But you can be proactive.

Some large corporations have discrete in-house teams whose sole job is issues and crisis management. In some instances the responsibility for issues management is devolved to a consultancy.

Many organisations don't have the budget for this and so need a work-manlike practical strategy to handle issues in-house. If you are responsible for issues management on a day-to-day basis within your organisation, I offer you the following checklist – this can be tailored to suit your resources. You may need to outsource some of the elements if you do not have the right skills or resources in-house; again this will be based on priorities.

Intelligence – gather it

Assemble past commentary and evidence on the issue including:

- Research and reports – government, scientific, opinion polls

- Media coverage – press, broadcast, Internet

- Net coverage – from newsgroups, chatrooms, online competitor press offices etc.

Over an agreed period (e.g. one year/five years):

- Arrange for frequent monitoring – this could be as frequent as every morning and afternoon (including weekends) – some issues need weekly monitoring, very few can be monitored effectively at less frequent intervals

- Analyse commentary – Look for patterns

- Messages – what is said to and what is being understood by the target audiences?

- Friends and foes – who is supportive, who is critical? Look especially at pressure groups – never underestimate their PR professionalism and media clout

- Seasonality – is there a time of year when this issue is 'hot'?

- Regionality – which parts of the country/globe are most inter-ested/affected?

Messages – agree them

- Try to keep these to a minimum – say three to four at the most

- Write these in layman's language – avoid jargon and science speak

- Get them onto a pocket-sized card for spokespeople

- Circulate these widely, adapting delivery to suit the audience

- Update frequently

Materials – create them

- Create support collateral

- Question and answer documents (Q&A) – a basic tool for the management of issues, asking every question a journalist might ask, particularly the difficult ones, and constructing the corporate answer – this document is then circulated to all spokespeople and may also be edited and used with other targets. The key messages should feature strongly. The Q&A may also be cut down to produce a FAQ (frequently asked questions) which could be edited for wide distribution and posted on the website

- Holding statements – on the issue which are updated regularly as the issue develops

- Supporting documentation – the organisation's own reports and papers about the issue, which can be used in discussions with journalists. Make sure they are e-mailable

- Background press materials – which should already be created and available for day-to-day media work and which may be posted in your online press office

Issues management team and spokespeople – select them

- Identify your issues management team – this should include:
    - Chief executive/Chairman/Managing director
    - PR/Communications director
    - Relevant members of the senior management team with particular knowledge of and/or responsibility for each given issue
    - External consultants, media handling advisers, press office, web master

- Select spokespeople – choose three or four – I would recommend:
    - The most senior person – e.g. CEO/MD
    - The most knowledgeable person – e.g. scientist, expert
    - The most genuine person – e.g. anyone who is sincere, authentic, takes a brief well and who could be the public face of the organisation
    - An independent spokesperson who could act as an advocate if the going gets tough

- Use materials to brief them

- Put spokespeople through their paces with presentation skills and media training focusing on the issue – include simulated interviews – press, TV, radio. Make sure they cut out any jargon

Internal communications – do it

- Make sure your own people – and perhaps national account managers, customers, suppliers and others closely involved or directly affected third parties – know what is going on and understand the key messages

- Do you need to communicate with colleagues and contacts around the world or is this simply a domestic issue?

- Keep them posted by e-mail, intranet, extranet

Tactics – use them

- Look for and create opportunities to make your point assertively – conferences, speaker platforms, features, chat shows and documentaries

Of course there may be instances where you judge that it is better to take a reactive rather than proactive stance – in which case refrain from proactive tactics and simply respond where necessary.

If you get your issues management right, not only is your reputation protected but you may also help to enhance your organisation's standing and develop a profile for your spokespeople as experts and commentators.

Crisis management

Many of the principles for issues management are carried into crisis management – but there are some additional strategic considerations:

Statements – write them

- In crisis management you need to get a basic statement together immediately which covers facts and may also include key messages. This should be available in printed format and also for electronic transmission. You will need to update the statement frequently as more information becomes available. The first time a statement goes out it is likely to be very short containing the basic facts only. This should be updated after the crisis management team meet to decide strategy

- What are the key facts?
  - What happened, when did it take place, where did it happen and who is involved?
  - The questions 'why' and 'how' something happened may have to be left while any investigation takes place

- Involve and negotiate with insurers and legal advisers. There can be considerable tension here about making public statements which may communicate what you need to say but which could imply acceptance of responsibility when no-one yet knows who is to blame. Keep in mind your objective – to protect and repair the reputation of the organisation with its target audiences – and use this as a yardstick when working with other advisers.

- Demonstrate your concern and give reassurance

- Tell people what action you are now taking – the management team are meeting now, there will be an investigation, a review of procedures, practical actions – anything which demonstrates that you are taking this seriously and doing something about it

- Use an unblemished record to underpin messages that this is a one-off, your organisation is not a past offender

- Let people know where and when further information will be available

- Direct people to your website for more information

Target audiences – identify them

- Agree priority targets – these may include:
    - Emergency services: police, fire, hospital, ambulance
    - Those immediately affected – e.g. involved parties' families and colleagues
    - Staff, customers, retailers, suppliers, legal advisers, insurers
    - Local MPs, local community
    - Media – local, regional, national, international
    - The general public
    - Decide who should contact each target group and what briefing materials and which channel they should use

Crisis team – assemble them

- This may be the issues management team but may also include other specialists, for example:
    - Operational experts
    - Health and safety experts
    - Site management and security teams
- Get them together as soon as possible preferably on the crisis site but in a private and quiet room where they can discuss strategy

Crisis management strategy – agree it

- Examine the nature of the crisis by asking the following questions:
    - Is there a more fundamental problem?
    - Are we at fault?
    - Is there an inherent weakness that makes us vulnerable?
    - How can we correct this?
    - If we can't, how can we prepare for a similar situation?
    - Is there more to come?
    - What is the worst-case scenario?
    - What will the target audience think/feel?
    - What are the timing implications?

- What is at stake regarding our reputation?

- Are there any advocates willing to speak for us?

- Are there any third parties involved?

- Is this a fragment of a bigger story?

- Can the crisis be contained?

- What action do we need to take now?

- Who will take it?

- When will we meet next?

Communications strategy – agree it

- Decide on your action plan by asking the following questions:

  - How proactive/reactive do we need to be?

  - What targets do we need to communicate with and how shall we accomplish this?

  - What media need to be briefed?

  - How do we do it?
    - written
    - e-mail/webcast
    - press conference
    - one-to-one press briefings

  - What do we post on the web immediately?

  - Who fronts for the organisation?

  - What do they say?

- If a press conference is required prepare media briefing packs containing:

  - The most current statement

  - Backgrounders on the organisation including: history, aims, objectives, major documents (e.g. annual report); financial position

  - Policy statements

  - Biographies of spokespeople and other board directors

  - Visuals if required or requests for photography/filming

- Select sites and brief site managers immediately – photographers and film crews will head straight for crisis sites without asking for permission
- Digital photography – e.g. sites, products, workforce, customers
- Video footage – Beta/VHS tape.

Practical issues – resolve them

- Crisis HQ

- Don't use the Chief Executive's office – create a dedicated space as the PR needs to be able to walk in at any moment.

- Try to locate the HQ close to or on the crisis site – have an emergency communication kit ready to roll for crises 'on location' and check it is up-to-date – web enabled mobile phone, Internet ready laptop with background press releases loaded and ready to e-mail, digital camera, portable printer, headed paper, corporate literature and backgrounders – remember mains cables, rechargers or spare batteries for electronic equipment

- Make sure the room has ISDN lines, phones, e-mail and web access

- Consider extra resourcing needs for the crisis HQ including staffing to cope 24 hours seven days a week. Make sure there are flipcharts, markers, blu-tac and refreshments available at all times.

Internal communications – brief people

- Your staff are your best and closest ambassadors. Keep them aware of developments as they occur

- As far as media is concerned, staff should be briefed as part of their induction that all media calls should be passed to the press office. Switchboard operators have a particular role to play in media management during a crisis

- Give switchboard staff briefing and instructions for media calls

- Pass media to in-house or external press office

- Use a media enquiry form (see p106) if staff end up taking a media call e.g. out-of-hours and pass to crisis team immediately.

Issues and crisis management training

Depending on budget consider the following to sharpen your issue and crisis handling skills:

- External courses on issues and crisis management – which may give you additional perspectives on the subject and which usually include relevant case histories

- In-house training – for PR and management teams who would be responsible for handling an issue or crisis. Useful as a team building exercise particularly if the issues and crisis team is drawn from disparate parts of the organisation or several sites are involved

- Media training for spokespeople – preferably with some input from or interviews with a working journalist. Can be held on site or in studio and would cover TV, radio, studio and down the line interviews and sound bites

- Regular 'road testing' for spokespeople – simulated and surprise media interviews on the phone with a 'journalist' – with feedback and suggestions for improvement

- Crisis simulation – to test the processes on site. May also include a simulated press conference.

Issues and crisis management and external consultants

There are times when an organisation simply cannot handle its own issues and crisis management. Maybe the in-house team is too small, they don't have this sort of experience, they are too busy on other projects or are on holiday or maternity leave, they just need some expert independent, external reality checking.

If you accept that issues and crisis management is a vital part of reputation management – and therefore the PR function – and you know or suspect that you will need an external consultant if the going gets tough, then get them in **now**. You may already use a consultancy – as a rule it's usually best to use existing partners, providing they have top up issue and crisis management capabilities as they will know your organisation and sector already. They may have indeed included a contingency for issues and crisis management as part of their overall PR planning and budgeting.

But don't wait until the issues are smothering you or the crisis has broken. It's just too late. If you are making a new appointment, get someone on board who understands the nature of your industry or sector and who has had experience dealing with your sort of issues and crises. Involve them in the planning stage, have short but regular update meetings. Pay them a retainer if you have to so that they are on call when you need them.

There are a number of consultancies which specialise in issues and crisis management. It may be worth considering one of these if you have a particular need where this sort of specialist support will deliver added value. Otherwise full service consultancies and corporate/public affairs consultancies usually have senior consultants with issues and crisis management experience. It's a question of shopping around to find the best fit. As far as fees are concerned, issues and crisis management has higher value attached to it and so daily or hourly rates are likely to be higher than you might expect to pay for a straightforward consumer, business-to-business or corporate campaign.

One final point

Clients and colleagues often ask me what about a crisis manual? Surely we need one?

Not necessarily. There was a time when it seemed sacrilegious to make such a suggestion. Ten years ago most in-house PR professionals had one of these weighty tomes on their shelves. Many PR consultants made a stack of money selling them to clients – and I have helped to write one or two of the things in the past.

The 'thud factor' of the crisis manual was used to prove to the anally retentive and disbelievers that this was a really serious subject and not one that could be treated lightly. Luckily we don't need to sell the concept as hard as we used to. Management teams generally acknowledge that issue and crisis management is vital and we all know what happens when organisations get it wrong.

Crisis manuals once tried to include every scenario that might befall an organisation – staff abusing vulnerable residents, fires at warehouses, the chief executive having an inappropriate relationship with the chairman's son, computer systems going down – and had ten pages of instructions about how to deal with each crisis. Some weren't crises at all and many scenarios were the product of feverish brainstorms held under pressure late at night. Inevitably the crisis that did occur varied wildly from the imagined scenario, so much so that the template proved little more than useless.

Manuals became unusable and unwieldy because they tried to combine procedural instruction with communications priorities. There is undoubtedly a place for procedures manuals but these are quite different to quick response communications plans which need to swing into action immediately.

We are also working faster and more remotely and we can't carry a 300 page manual round with us – although this could now be loaded onto a laptop, disk or CD-ROM. But there isn't the time to plough through an encyclopaedia when news is breaking by the second on the Internet.

And crisis manuals need updating. Many of those dusty old volumes had contact details and names of folk who had long since left the company or who had been transferred to Bogota. The bigger the organisation, the bigger the admin problem.

The truth is that, as I said at the outset, it is all down to planning in advance and then performing on the day. If you go through the issue audit you will identify those areas where you are most vulnerable and where planning is necessary. Then follow through the processes I outline above, making sure that issues and crisis management is alive in your organisation, not something you did once and filed away, just in case. You should end up with holding statements and questions and answers – which should be lodged on a secure intranet and be accessible from remote locations, including for the press team, from home.

As far as crisis manuals are concerned, I suggest you simply produce and circulate the following three pieces of paper to the relevant people on a need to know basis. Try to produce then in a filofax or similar compact format so they can carry them at all times. Update and reissue them every other month and be absolutely methodical about this.

1. A key contact list which has phone numbers, including home and mobiles, and e-mail addresses – if you can, organise this list so that spokespeople's responsibility is clear and you can call the right person quickly when there is an urgent media query or opportunity.

2. An issue and crisis communication action checklist – compile your own based on the checklists in this chapter. Try not to exceed a couple of sides of A4 paper.

3. Key messages – as discussed earlier.

Evaluating issues and crisis management

So it's all over... how did you do?

First of all it is a mistake to think it is all over. Issues run and run and may come to the fore at any time. Follow-up news coverage of the results of an inquest, public inquiry or private prosecution all serve to resurrect the memories of the crisis. For those worst affected it never goes away. One year, ten years, twenty years after the event and parents may still be grieving for a drowned teenager, a woman may still look in a mirror and see the scars from the train crash, a widow leaves flowers where the bomb went off. Anniversaries make strong human-interest news stories.

This is a reality and you need to plan for it. Make sure you have a statement ready about how things have progressed since that time, what action you have taken and what good news came from bad.

But you can evaluate the process. You can review qualitatively the way you handled an issue or crisis. Did you follow the process? Did you get some reflections from a trusted journalist? What were the outcomes? Should you review the issues and crisis management procedures? This will tell you if the processes and procedures are right for your organisation and whether your team is working well.

You can qualitatively and quantitatively evaluate media coverage. Where did it appear? How fast did the story travel in all media – Internet, radio, TV, press? This will tell you what the media has said about you – good and bad – how big the story was, how many viewers, listeners and readers may have registered your organisation's name and involvement in the story and, vitally, did your messages get across?

You can track sales figures and share prices. These will tell you whether there has been any commercial impact. You can also track correspondence into the organisation to gauge how individuals, perhaps representing interested groups and other organisations, have responded.

For the PR professional the key issue is whether your reputation has been damaged or enhanced in the long-term by these events. To be absolutely certain, you must look at continuous tracking. To do this really well and to be able to extrapolate the most value from the data, put monitoring in place now and measure at regular intervals, before, during and after the events in question. This may take the form of qualitative or quantitative studies among one or several key stakeholders, perhaps those most vital to your organisation. Only then can you be certain you have met your objectives.

Checklist

Issues and crisis management

Do

✓ Plan

✓ Communicate

✓ Communicate simply – cut the jargon

✓ Get management buy-in

✓ Get in help – more in-house resources or a consultancy – if you need to

✓ Train the team together

✓ Demonstrate that public interest/safety is the main issue and empathise with the people who have been affected

✓ Look for cooperation and conciliation

✓ Learn from the experience – change working practices, review and track reputation

✓ Work fast – viral communications means the story can be worldwide in ten minutes – or less

Don't

✗ Wait for it – whatever it is – to happen

✗ Bury your head in the sand or say 'no comment'

✗ Muddy communications with irrelevant jargon, management-speak or too many facts and figures

✗ Make it just a PR only issue (it's a much wider issue)

X   Struggle on with inadequate resources

X   Come over as an arrogant organisation with commercial concerns as the key driver

X   Engage in conflict or head-to-heads with victims and relatives, media or opponents

X   Put it in a box at the end of the day and forget about it

X   Put it off until tomorrow

chapter eleven

Public relations specialisms

Introduction

While general principles apply across the board and planning is the same whatever the sector, there are a number of specialist areas in public relations where special consideration and particular techniques are applied to give greater 'bang for bucks'.

Some consultancies have recognised the importance of this expertise to clients seeking particular types of support and have responded by either concentrating exclusively on one industry or sector – for example healthcare or consumer – or, as is usually the case with larger consultancies, by setting up a number of practice groups where discrete teams offer in-depth knowledge and understanding of different sectors and/or specific target audiences.

Here we look at the major specialist practice areas and outline the key points of difference which distinguish one from another.

Business-to-business

Business-to-business (B2B) campaigns focus on developing the relationship between organisations who provide products or services to other businesses, for example a supplier of bulk fuels to the logistics industry or stationery to offices. Consequently B2B campaigns are often strategically linked to the sales strategy. When developing a B2B programme, it pays to take a highly pragmatic approach, focusing on understanding and solving business problems. The communications objectives will need to complement the corporate and sales and marketing objectives. The B2B campaign should also dovetail into internal relations programmes so that your own people are aware of business developments and issues or crisis management plans.

Unique features of B2B

B2B programmes differ from other PR programmes in several important ways:

- The total number of potential buyers may be very small, for example the supplier of bulk fuels to the logistics industry may only have ten to twenty targets in his/her sights – e.g. supermarket chains, logistics groups and major bus companies

- There are likely to be a finite number of targets – it might even be possible to pinpoint named individuals in target organisations

- For these reasons, the most appropriate method for reaching these targets may be via face-to-face communication techniques and highly targeted, low circulation specialist media

- The sales value is likely to be high

- When the sales value is high, the decision to buy takes longer to reach and may involve a number of parties. Take for example the decision to switch from diesel to an alternative fuel by a supermarket group for its lorry fleet – this would require capital expenditure and would therefore need ratification from the fleet manager, the regional manager, the fuel buyer, the finance director, the logistics director, or even the managing director or chief executive

- When these targets buy, they buy perhaps once a year, by contract following negotiation and in bulk. For the rest of the year the product or service is likely to be at the back of the mind – unless, of course, things go wrong.

Elements in a B2B campaign

In order to mount a successful B2B PR campaign, you need reasons to talk to customers and to the media. One or more of the following elements are crucial to give you that momentum:

- The introduction of entirely new technology/a new sales process or business philosophy which the stakeholder has not previously been exposed to

- Product launches/relaunches/significant upgrades

- Winning new contracts

- Spokespeople who are experts on the market

- Promoting success using case histories

- Promoting the organisation's services to customers

- Promoting new people or consultants

- Office/factory/premises openings, moves or closures

- Diversity into another market or sector

- Pre or post acquisition reassurance

- Product withdrawal – and the positive action being taken thereafter.

Consumer

Whether you are a PR professional, entrepreneur, managing director, student or full-time mother, you are a consumer. We all buy food, drink, shampoo, CDs, books, socks, mortgages, holidays, mobile phones, digital TVs, PCs and software etc.

Consumer PR is probably the longest established 'specialism' in the industry and indeed for the general public and the uninitiated PR *is* consumer PR. But it has historically suffered from a poor image, as the 'fluffy' end of the market. At one stage consumer PR was dominated by the doyennes of the industry, chain smoking designer dressed Sloane Rangers partying their way from publishing house to publishing house, holding lavish drinks parties to celebrate just about anything, from a new store opening to the launch of a new sandwich spread and every-thing in between. A thick address book, a permanently engaged telephone and a pile of press cuttings were enough and everything was done on the hoof with gut feel being the main driver.

There are still a few operators who fit this description – and fantasti-cally successful they are too. But consumer PR is now as meticulously well planned and as rigorously evaluated as any other PR discipline. With the fragmentation of the media and the increasing ability to define with absolute clarity the type of consumer you want to reach, consumer PR is more considered and scientific than it used to be and has more in common with direct marketing than might be expected. Indeed marketing strategies for consumer products and services often include direct marketing, advertising and sales promotion working alongside consumer public relations. Synergy between the disciplines is vital.

Consumer PR campaigns may also work alongside or feed other areas. A consumer campaign for a new range of saucepans, targeting newly-weds, first time home buyers and keen home cooks might also include an opinion formers campaign, targeting home economists and food writers; a business-to-business campaign, targeting retailers and whole-salers; and an internal campaign, targeting the workforce.

Defining the consumer

The 'general public' is rarely a realistic target – it is simply too broad and amorphous. Perhaps the only exception is the public information campaign, for example for the census or self-assessment tax returns, which have very substantial budgets and which must attempt to inform every adult in the country about a change in legislation or policy.

You need to break down consumers into prioritised groups. In this way you can plan activities which are targeted, tailored and affordable. When planning consumer campaigns, it is essential to look at as much consumer research as possible, including readership/audience profiles.

Sticking with the example of a new range of saucepans, the broad stakeholder group might be 25-44 year old men and women, B, C1. However by interrogating research and looking at consumer data, more focused subgroups emerge – newlyweds, first time home buyers, keen home cooks – who are much more likely to be considering purchasing new saucepans.

Once you have agreed subgroups, use this list of ten questions to help get a picture of the consumer(s) so you understand what makes your stakeholders tick and how, where and when you might reach them using PR techniques:

1. What life stage are they at?

2. Where do they live?

3. What sort of work do they do?

4. What are their values and priorities?

5. What are their concerns and issues?

6. How do they spend their leisure time?

7. What sort of spending habits do they have?

8. What media do they read/watch/listen to?

9. How much and when do they use the Internet?

10. How do they use our own and our competitors products/services?

Consumer PR tactics

Tactic

Media relations	Set up a press office offering a reactive service (samples provision, response to media enquiries etc.) and managing proactive campaigns

Editorial promotions

Working with publications, TV programmes, radio stations and websites selected to reach defined targets

- Reader offers – giveaways and samples

- Competitions – involving the reader with a substantial main prize, product and branded merchandise

- Advertorials – half advertisement and half editorial and often flagged '*advertising (or advertisement) feature*' – these are created in the editorial style of the magazine and are designed to be involving and participative

Cause related marketing campaign

See chapter six

Sponsorship

See below

Face-to-face communications

Also see chapter thirteen

- Launch events – for the media and opinion formers

- Roadshows – in shopping malls and high streets, supermarket car parks, railway concourses, county shows, regionally or nationally or in specific regions, with a mobile trailer/stand – exhibit/give information/give away samples, tastings, literature etc.

- Exhibitions (e.g. Ideal Home, Mother and Baby Shows, Heath and Beauty Shows, The Boat Show etc.) – as roadshows but one selected event with a permanent stand for the duration of the show

- Awards schemes – with a ceremony plus lunch, drinks or dinner

Corporate PR

If you accept that public relations is about reputation, then perhaps corporate PR is the purest expression of this. Corporate PR is the deliberate and planned management of the reputation of an organisation, usually over months and years. The organisation benefits from positive perceptions among and support from its target audiences. This, in turn, creates a favourable climate for operating, where positive public opinion works in the organisation's favour.

Before embarking on a proactive corporate PR programme, the organisation should examine itself closely to ensure that:

- It is being managed effectively

- The man or woman at the top is an effective, respected figurehead for the organisation

- It is perceived well at the present time

- There is a sound ethical review process which feeds into management

- Quality goods and services are being produced

- Customers' needs are being listened to – and complaints are tackled quickly and effectively.

If the organisation cannot satisfy itself on any of these points, it should act to improve the situation. No PR professional should think that corporate PR can be used as whitewash, to cover the cracks or divert attention from important issues which the organisation should face up to and address. The messages should be truthful, with the emphasis on disclosure not concealment. This engenders trust and tells your stakeholders that the organisation plays a straight bat, puts people first and believes in being open and honest.

These days corporate PR is often inextricably linked with public affairs and financial PR – stakeholders overlap, particularly in the case of listed companies, where shareholders are an important focus for communications and where opinion can literally make or break a company.

Stakeholders for corporate PR

- **Employees** – recognised as ambassadors for every organisation

- **Shareholders** – where faith in the organisation and an understanding of its performance is paramount

- **Customers** – whose loyalty is key

- **Pressure groups** – who are themselves highly organised and professional and who will target an organisation that appears to be behaving covertly or improperly

- **Trade unions, politicians and civil servants** – who need to feel assured that the organisation is responsible and trustworthy, particularly if it is applying for regulatory or legal change

- **Banks, city institutions, financial analysts** – who may recommend the organisation to investors and institutions

- **Trade associations** – whose support may be valuable at time of crisis

- **Local community** – the source of the workforce; the organisation is perhaps a major employer and goodwill and support will enable it to continue operating smoothly.

Planning corporate PR

Planning a corporate PR programme is much the same as planning any other PR programme. Research among the stakeholders will uncover issues and may even reveal that there are messages that the audiences need or want to hear about the organisation.

A useful adjunct in the planning process is the pros and cons list – your summation of the positive and negative perceptions which currently exist about the organisation, derived from both qualitative and quantitative research among the target audience(s). This list will help you pinpoint the problems, agree priorities and devise communications strategies which enhance the positives and address the negatives.

Following are two examples. The first is a company in the telecommunications business, the second is a not for profit organisation, with a residential care facility.

Example 1: An international telecoms company

Positive perceptions	Negative perceptions
• Major UK brand name	• Doesn't listen to customers – too big and remote
• Been around a long time	• Too slow to adapt in a fast changing market
• Major employer	• Too expensive – competitors are offering better value for money
• Skilled workforce	• Poor management has led to poor financial performance

Example 2: A charitable organisation

Positive perceptions	Negative perceptions
• Recognised by World Health Organisation as a centre of excellence	• Old fashioned
• Quality of care exceptionally high	• Parochial
• Sound management	• Not mainstream
• Well-known locally	• Low awareness outside home territory

Arrogance, complacency and a cavalier attitude towards customers seem to be the main issues for the first company, while the second organisation is exceptionally worthy but sleepy, seemingly stuck in a backwater and needing to be dragged kicking and screaming into the twenty first century.

Corporate PR techniques

The emphasis is on regular and consistent communications so, dependent on budget, you might choose one or a number of the following:

- Website and web based communications – including e-mail news bulletins (but never 'spam' people with unsolicited e-mails. Always ask first before adding anyone's e-mail address to an automatic mail out system)

- Design and corporate ID – the impact of good corporate design is obvious and the PR practitioner may take responsibility for the development and application of the corporate identity

- Research studies – involving the stakeholders or in response to a particular issue, to tackle issues or to strengthen perceptions in an area where you already have a positive profile or recognised expertise.

- Publications and reports – which can be used to demonstrate authority on a subject

- Face-to-face meetings, seminars and events – where in-depth dialogue can take place, particularly useful when gauging opinion

- Cause related marketing campaigns – in partnership with a charitable body or not for profit organisation, where the association will enhance the perceptions of both parties and may have commercial benefits

- Sponsorships – mainly in sports or arts where an organisation can derive considerable benefits from being seen to be active in a specific area

- PR-led advertising – designed to enhance/repair the reputation of an organisation, not to sell specific products or services.

Financial PR

Financial PR is a highly valued and specialised type of public relations; valued because of the influence it can have on a company's share price and specialised because it requires in-depth knowledge of how the financial world works, including knowledge of the regulations and laws which govern the way information is delivered. This includes the Stock Exchange Regulations, The Companies Act, the Takeover Code and so on. An understanding of the laws relating to the release of information which could affect the share price or the market as a whole is also crucial.

As mentioned above, financial and corporate public relations are frequently interrelated given a main common objective is the creation and protection of corporate reputation. A positive reputation is vital in attracting investment. Given the close links between politics and industry, public affairs may also dovetail into the financial PR plan. The financial PR adviser or investor relations manager, whether in-house or consultant, is usually a member of the elite team comprising of other professional advisers, including lawyers and financiers.

Financial PR is distinct from financial services marketing, where financial products – like mortgages, pensions and PEPs – are presented to a mainly consumer audience.

An important feature of financial PR is the specialised group of target audiences it seeks to communicate with.

Target audiences	
Analysts	Financial and stockbrokers' analysts undertake research and make recommendations to investors and advisers – their recommendations are trusted and acted upon
Institutional shareholders	Large pension funds and insurance companies are major investors
City institutions and organisations	Stockbrokers, accountants, management consultancies, lawyers and merchant banks act for and advise the institutional shareholders – their opinions carry weight
Shareholders	Your own current shareholders and potential shareholders
Influencers	Government (Westminster and Brussels)
The media reaching these groups	*The Financial Times*, www.ft.com business and financial sections of the Daily and Sunday broadsheets, Business journals e.g. *Investors Weekly*. Journals produced by institutions e.g. *Director* (for the Institute of Directors) online and cable investment channels (e.g. Bloomburgs)

Financial PR – the main events and tactics

Financial 'event'	PR tactics
Announcements	
• Announcements relating to financial performance are required to be made by public companies twice a year – the *preliminary* and *interim* results (preliminary at the end of the financial year and interim at the half year)	• Advertising – of results, chairman's statement etc. – in the press and on the website
	• Media relations
	– Media training for spokespeople
• The *annual report and accounts* and the *Annual General Meeting* are very important points in the year – it is here that the management reports on the successes of the past year and outlines plans for the future	– Press releases
	– One-to-one briefings for selected journalists, either face-to-face or on the phone
	– Press conferences
• *Prior notice* is the announcement made to the Stock Exchange in advance of the publication of results	*NB Timing is crucial re closed periods etc. again to avoid breaching regulations or breaking the law*
Flotation	
• Raising capital by issuing shares	• Devising a communications plan attracting would-be investors
	• The production of a prospectus
	• Advertising the prospectus
	• Media briefings
	• Briefing institutions and analysts
	• Press advertising

Public affairs
- Takeover judged contrary to public interest
- Company is subject of hostile bid
- Redundancies as a result of collapse of business, consolidation, factory closure etc.
- Industry issues, including regulatory matters
- Interface with a Government department which is a customer

- Communications with MPs
- Submissions to Office of Fair Trading
- New Competition Act and Competition Commission

Corporate literature
- Website
- Corporate brochure
- Annual report (must include mandatory elements)
- Takeover bids/defence documents

- Management of design, print and production
- Copywriting – particularly statements, background information and feature pieces
- Use within briefing packs to all targets

Crisis management
- Profit warnings
- Management difficulties
- Hostile takeover bid
- Pressure group targeting

- Press office management
- Issue and crisis management

Healthcare

Healthcare public relations encompasses a broad spectrum of activity, which is getting broader all the time as regulations and healthcare systems change.

Like financial PR, this is an area where the planning process and use of PR techniques must take into account regulations set by a number of bodies. These include the Department of Health, the Medicines Control Agency (MCA), the Association of the British Pharmaceutical Industry (ABPI) and the Proprietary Association of Great Britain (PAGB), as well as the bodies who regulate healthcare professionals, such as the General Medical Council.

There are traditionally two types of healthcare PR – ethical and consumer. Even this is now blurring with the birth of functional foods and direct to consumer (DTC) medicines (see page 164). Medical education is often considered a third type – this straddles both areas and covers communication programmes with health professionals designed to help them understand the use and relevance of particular diagnoses, drugs and treatments.

Ethical healthcare public relations

Ethical healthcare covers drugs and medical services that are only available to consumers via prescription from a doctor or are provided in hospital. This is regardless of whether the delivery is through the NHS or privately. It is termed ethical not because all other healthcare PR is unethical but because it is bound by strict regulation.

Anyone working in this field, whether in-house or consultancy, should go on an induction course with the ABPI and have regular refreshers. Indeed it is often stipulated as a mandatory requirement by pharmaceutical companies when employing a consultancy, as the client is liable for any breach of regulations which result from PR activity undertaken on their behalf.

While you don't need a medical or scientific background to become a skilled ethical healthcare PR practitioner, the ability to interrogate data or research studies is a definite advantage. But plenty of people working in this field don't have science degrees or medical qualifications and have learnt the business from the inside, for example in a hospital press office.

The objectives for ethical healthcare public relations can range from helping to prepare the ground for a new drug launch and creating an education programme for healthcare professionals on a particular disease area to extending the lifecycle of existing brands.

Sample PR techniques include:

Advisory panels	Made up of representatives from the medical professions, usually those specialising in or with an interest in a particular disease area. Paid an honourarium for attending a set number of confidential meetings a year and they usually sign a confidentiality agreement, ensuring non-disclosure to competitors. Offer advice to the company and act as sounding board for ideas and plans
Conferences and special events	Supporting a company's attendance at relevant medical meetings; organising satellite seminars or press events or possibly bulletins to relevant medics unable to attend
Bulletins and newsletters	Directed at key healthcare professionals most involved in the recommendation or delivery of the company's drug or treatment
Professional education	To assist healthcare professionals in diagnosing and treating particular conditions and/or using a particular drug which may have a new treatment regime, new treatment indication or delivery method. Compliance with continuing education is now a requirement for all health professionals and such programmes can be designed to offer accreditation, making them more attractive to take up. Techniques can be highly interactive and involve CD-ROMs and the Internet, as well as paper-based training manuals

Patient advocacy	Creating links with the relevant patient group. This could be in the form of sponsored materials or activity (such as funding a vital helpline for sufferers) or in working with the group to create consensus guidelines on treatment or care for the disease concerned. This can be a highly effective way of reaching target consumers within the regulations and enhancing corporate reputation as well
Media relations	Ranging from promoting new published studies to supporting a disease awareness campaign through a patient group. Companies cannot advertise or promote products but they may provide information to the media providing it is balanced and objective e.g. Uprima

The regulations, which public relations practitioners must abide by, are there to prevent pharmaceutical companies from trying to influence consumers without the advice and intervention of a qualified medical practitioner. For example, at present companies cannot advertise or promote in any other way details of their drug and what it claims to do direct to consumers, for example through features in women's magazines.

However, things are changing, following the arrival of direct to consumer (DTC) advertising in the USA. Although this is not legal yet in the UK and Europe, companies are looking to adapt such an approach to fit the current rules, particularly if a drug is the leading product in a particular field and the firm's name is synonymous with a particular therapeutic area. In this case, it may be possible to look at disease awareness promotions and education, bearing discrete corporate branding.

Consumer healthcare public relations

Consumer healthcare covers both product PR and general health promotion targeted at consumers. Health professionals are usually also a stakeholder group – most frequently pharmacists and nurses but also doctors and specialist professions such as dentists, chiropodists, physiotherapists and occupational health officers.

PR for Over the Counter (OTC) products

In this category, there are two types of products:

- 'P' medicines – available only from pharmacists and under their supervision. This means that a pharmacy assistant should not actually sell them across the counter to you without the knowledge of the pharmacist. Medicines often become 'P' products after applying to switch from POM (Prescription Only Medicine) status when the MCA considers that consumers will be able to take them safely and according to instructions without the supervision of a doctor. Examples of products which have 'switched' in recent years are Zovirax cold sore cream and Canestan treatment for thrush.

- GSL (General Sales List) products – these can be bought off the shelf in a supermarket but may still be medicines, for example Alka-Seltzer and Nurofen.

Although not bound by so many regulations, there are still some specific guidelines which anyone wanting to create and implement a consumer healthcare PR programme for either category should be aware of. For example, you cannot sample any medicinal product to the public or make a direct claim that the product cures a condition or illness. Any statements about what it does must mirror its product licence, granted by the MCA.

The Proprietary Association of Great Britain (PAGB) represents over 95% of manufacturers of OTC products and provides the industry with a self-regulatory code. It has a set of guidelines for both PR and advertising and, like the ABPI, it offers regular induction and refresher courses.

Techniques are much the same as those used in general consumer PR, as long as the rules on what you can say and how you can say it are followed and pre-approved by the PAGB. All new ideas and copy for press releases or consumer literature should be passed by the PAGB before they are produced, whether you are working in-house or in consultancy.

Health education

These campaigns are often undertaken by pharmaceutical companies, charities, pressure groups, professional organisations and by the Government. Recent examples include the sun awareness campaign to help prevent skin cancer and the programme promoting breast screening. The aim of these programmes is to change behaviour and this is a long-term objective, more complex to measure than simply evaluating whether sales of a cough medicine met March sales targets. As a result, programmes are often planned to run over several years so that change can be properly benchmarked and measured over time using market research.

Internal communications

Employees are a special and important stakeholder group. Good communication within an organisation enables amazing things to be achieved. This is not only because people need to know what is going on to do their job better, they are also motivated by positive messages, they understand the brand and act as ambassadors every day. If people understand why they are doing what they are doing and how this contributes to the whole, their interest is engaged and they are more likely to give of their best. Productivity increases, it's easier to recruit higher calibre people and those who join, stay. There are plenty of reasons why internal communications make sense.

> **Central objectives for internal communications**
>
> - To ensure information flows quickly and effectively through the organisation so that practices, policies and procedures are understood and acted upon
>
> - To encourage and motivate people so that they feel truly involved and give of their best

In the UK, the Investors in People Standard places great importance on internal communications. Indeed the Standard can only be achieved when a high level of internal communications is taking place in the organisation – this points towards the internal communications strategy being determined at the highest level by the management team. Inductions, job descriptions and appraisals are all channels of communication and the information gathered as a result of undertaking these activities can be enlightening, prompting new thinking or new policies which make a difference to the bottom line.

Internal communications is used to help the process of change management – and constant change is a daily reality. It can also help to unify a diverse organisation and pull people together in times of crisis. Internal communications sometimes stands alone as a function in large organisations. Otherwise it may straddle PR and HR and may be the responsibility of both... or either! Internal communications sometimes sits beside corporate communications. Whatever the reporting line, the professional PR practitioner can add real value, by applying the principles of PR planning to ensure that the internal communications programme is true to the brand values and is as effective as possible. Don't cut the budget for internal communications if business takes a downturn – in fact invest more in internal communications in times of change to keep people onside and informed.

Planning internal communications

Using standard planning methods, an internal communications programme would commence with an audit, in this case an audit of employee attitudes. This could examine:

- How much is getting through to employees at present

- Whether the current communications channels are effective and the right people are involved

- Where and how employees get information – is it from their managers, chat on the shop floor, formal or informal lines, via notice boards or electronically?

- Employees' current opinions and attitudes

- What information employees would like that they currently don't have access to

- Is communication a two-way street? i.e. people's comments, ideas and suggestions reach management and are acted upon as much as messages from management are transmitted to employees.

Delivering information internally

Honesty and frankness are vital components in terms of the tone of all internal communications programmes. This is especially true during times of change or when bad news needs to be broken. The visibility of the man - or woman - at the top is vital and he/she may need to be counselled in terms of how to approach face-to-face communications with staff. Indeed there may be a need to train managers so that they learn effective ways to gather, edit and transmit information to employees.

Bad news should always be delivered face-to-face – never resort to e-mails, memos pinned to notice boards or dropped into in-trays – this is a sure-fire way to encourage gossip, rumours and bad feeling.

Delivering news face-to-face to a number of people needs careful planning. It is usually best handled as a cascade, commencing with meeting(s) involving the senior management team, followed by personal interviews with key managers and culminating with team briefings throughout the organisation. This can then be followed up with management bulletins, e-mails, information posted on the intranet, written memos, posters on notice boards and so on.

The language you use for internal communication will be determined by the corporate image, brand values and/or personality at the top of the organisation. As a rule informality and brevity are more effective and are reflective of a more honest and frank approach – and an honest and frank management team.

Finally timing and alignment with external relations plans is vital so the entire communications process works as a coherent whole.

What people want and need to know

- Information about the organisation and the department the person works in – productivity, new contracts, new people, new products, training courses.

- Work being done around the company – in other departments, other UK sites, overseas locations.

- Awards and accolades.

- Opportunities for personal development, training etc.

- Financial results – profitability, bonuses, and incentive schemes. In the charitable sector fundraising, campaign successes and grants.

- Policies – in writing, covering many different aspects of the organisation's activities (which may be delivered as a handbook or posted on your organisation's intranet).

- Information about working conditions – including disciplinary procedures, grievances, disputes, salary bands (if standard and published) etc.

- Heath and safety information – a legal requirement.

Internal communications tools

- Publications – a company policy document; an employee's handbook (frequently now delivered online, on disk or CD-ROM); works rules; managers' handbook; annual report (even if not a legal requirement this is a useful tool and can be used as the company brochure too); newsletters, magazines etc.

- Online communications – intranet and e-mails (particularly important for remote or home based colleagues).

- Team briefings, joint committees, regular briefing sessions.

- Special events – social occasions, awaydays, training workshops and courses.

- Incentive schemes.

- Corporate sponsorship or charity link up – that can involve the entire workforce.

Technology/ hi-tech/IT

In the twenty-first century, we are all consumers of technology at home for leisure and for business and in the workplace. High-tech/IT PR is now mainstream. Where once the focus was on trade and business communications, the IT sector now communicates with consumers via B2C (business-to-consumer) PR campaigns and understands the importance of corporate and financial relations and public affairs too, particularly where regulatory issues impact on a company's ability to conduct its business freely.

The definition of high-tech includes high-tech products and services, from Internet service providers to mobile phone companies, from software publishers to hi-fi manufacturers. Interestingly some practitioners do not include dot.coms in this grouping, unless the dot.com in question happens to offer high-tech products and services. Dot.coms are actually online organisations and businesses and so a dot.com may require corporate, financial, business-to-business, business-to-consumer, consumer, high-tech or any other type of PR support, depending on the sector they are operating in.

The PR planning process is essentially the same. Perhaps a little more time will need to be invested in learning about the products and services. Whether you are the in-house practitioner for a company in the high-tech sector or you are a consultant to a high-tech company, start by working on a broad understanding of how the company and the products or services work. You don't need to become an 'anorak' and know the minute technical detail – a savvy engineer or designer can give you that, especially one who has been media trained and understands that communication is more effective when it is jargon free. However, clients or colleagues often feel more comfortable with and confident in public relations practitioners who can talk-the-talk during business meetings and briefings, even if they are going to translate for external audiences.

Hi-tech media

The number of high-tech magazines is growing all the time and includes:

* Technology industry specific e.g. cable

* Product specific media e.g. software, home PC

* Titles for different industries using high-tech e.g. design business, small business, health service etc.

* Dealer magazines.

Hi-tech was, as might be expected, the first sector to utilise e-communications and e-media relations. For the practitioner working in this sector it is important to get the tone right when preparing media materials. This demands an understanding of the media and the ability to adapt the approach to match the writer and the reader. Specialist titles give all the technical details and use jargon and are written by knowledgeable journalists for knowledgeable enthusiasts. These journalists are not only highly tech-literate they are also early adopters of new concepts, products and services. Get these people close to your company by operating a lending service – get your product into their homes or offices and let them try the kit for themselves. This may encourage more quality in-depth coverage and will certainly build relationships.

The majority of media is written by and for people who need and want information but not the technical detail and who haven't got the time to code-break the jargon. Write simply and focus on the working benefits, rather than the operational features. Use photography which involves people and shows products in use rather than in a box – unless of course the design is so sexy (think about the i-Mac) that it speaks volumes.

Target audiences for high-tech PR

Users

- Customers – consumer, business (within businesses the owner-manager, the information technology manager or webmaster and the finance director as decision maker)

- Education – schools, colleges, universities, other learning providers

Distributors

- Retailers, dealers, wholesale trade, resellers

Business partners

- Employees – current and potential

- Suppliers

Recommenders

- Management consultants, systems management companies

Financial sector

- Current and potential investors, financial institutions

Checklist

✓ Understand the rules applicable to your own sector.

✓ Join relevant industry bodies and associations.

✓ Get to know the key media and named journalists in your specialist sector.

✓ Get external support and use experts who specialise in your sector where necessary.

chapter twelve

Public affairs

Introduction

As discussed in chapter two, public relations has been employed by successive governments, using public funds to educate, to inform and to change attitudes and behaviour. It has also been used for party political purposes, to engage and attract support and is particularly effective in local and national election campaigns.

Public affairs is now increasingly integrated with public relations. That doesn't mean that you don't need public affairs expertise – in fact quite the reverse is true, given the rules, regulations and complexities surrounding the political system. But more often than not the public affairs practitioner now works closely alongside his/her public relations colleague. Target groups interact and in order to manage the business environment it is important to ensure consistent communications. The government is also increasingly influenced not just by direct commercial lobbying but by a wide range of third parties – consumer groups, NGOs, think-tanks, the City, business organisations as well as, of course, the media. Political correspondents, leader-writers and columnists wield considerably more influence than obscure government backbenchers. Effective campaigning needs to recognise this and to include political media relations as a discrete element in planning. Modern lobbying is now frequently about building a coalition of supporters of and advocates for your cause. The first and most important step is to identify precisely the real influencers on any decision or policy and then to discover effective and legitimate ways of getting your messages across to them.

There are some specific rules and codes which must be adhered to by public affairs practitioners. The Association of Political and Parliamentary Consultants and the Public Relations Consultants Association have formulated a code of practice relating to disclosure of interests by those employed as political consultants. It is not permissible to lobby some parties directly, for example Department of Trade and Industry ministers about mergers and acquisitions or ministers whose departments are involved in procurement campaigns.

Ethical issues have also been widely debated in recent years. Access to privileged information, impropriety relating to payments and favours for services rendered – these issues have hit the headlines, involving individuals with political influence working with organisations who have commercial interests. The 1995 Nolan Report on standards in public life began the process of clarifying what is and what is not acceptable and MPs must declare any earnings derived from advising organisations. At the time of writing these issues are still being debated within the industry.

For those who adhere to the rules, public affairs strategies enable organisations to communicate effectively with all those who have an influence on the way the organisation is able to conduct itself or the way it is viewed. The effective use of public affairs techniques can help an organisation to influence public policy or possibly legislation. Public affairs can also support business objectives directly by, for example, securing an acquisition or a government contract, selling proactively to government, helping to raise awareness of an organisation's aims and objectives and achieving regulatory approval or fending off unwelcome regulatory action.

The concept of lobbying is accepted as an essential part of the democratic process, particularly given the increasing burden of legislation not only originating in the UK nationally and in the devolved administration in Scotland, Wales and Northern Ireland but also within the European Union. All sorts of organisations, from the farming community to energy companies, unions to charitable institutions, need to put their points of view across, to ensure their issues are on the political agenda and that they achieve a fair hearing to support their organisational objectives. A campaign may set out to change the political climate and may involve all levels of government, pressure and community groups, the media, other organisations here and even overseas – a point in case was the phenomenally successful campaign to ban the world-wide use of land mines.

In many organisations the management of the public affairs programme is the responsibility of a specialist in public or corporate affairs, whether that is an in-house practitioner or an independent consultant. Many of these specialists have worked in government themselves or are active in political circles.

Then there is the specialised jargon of Westminster (what exactly is an Early Day Motion and is it really significant?) but ultimately there is no real mystique to public affairs. It is all good common sense. The way to achieve real success in public affairs is to construct your case reasonably and clearly, to communicate this appropriately with those individuals who have a genuine interest in your organisation or the issue you are highlighting and to do this at the right time.

The four basic questions for the public relations practitioner – if he or she is not a public or corporate affairs specialist – are:

1. How do you plan a public affairs campaign?

2. Who are the political targets I need to build a relationship with and how should they be communicated with?

3. What do I need to know about political processes?

4. What tactics are most likely to achieve corporate objectives?

Definition

Public affairs – the planned management of public and political issues which may have an impact on the reputation, performance or licence to operate of any business or organisation.

Public affairs planning

In principle, a public affairs campaign is planned in much the same way as any other public relations campaign. In a broad sense you need to know the lie of the land and the political environment in which you are operating. This includes an understanding of what may affect your organisation in terms of the content of the manifestos of the main political parties and their policy making processes, the Queen's Speech at the opening of Parliament each year, the aims of the devolved administration in Scotland, Wales and Northern Ireland, the agenda in local government and the policies of the European institutions, particularly the Assembly and Commission in Brussels.

If you are a house builder you need to understand how the current administration views land use or how local policies might affect land value. A vaccine producer will be interested in public health policy and the potential effect on new product development programmes. A small business owner in Scotland will be concerned about employment law here and in Europe and the impact of any legislation on his or her expansion and recruitment plans. Is regulation on the agenda? Are there policies which will have a knock-on effect on the way your organisation operates, like regional development plans?

Audit

Planning starts with an audit of information on the issues and political developments which affect the organisation. This has become easier over the years with a more transparent democratic process, with televised proceedings and public access to political and legislative documentation. The skill here is identifying what is of real interest or significance from the plethora of official documentation produced every day. It is reasonably simple to track by using the Internet. You do not need to know every last parliamentary question or reference in debates. You could consider the following sources of information:

- Parliamentary and Assembly monitoring – for the House of Commons and the House of Lords in London, the Parliament in Edinburgh and the Assemblies in Cardiff and Stormont. Hansard has always been the bible for day-to-day reportage of proceedings in the House of Commons. Reports of proceedings and minutes from Select Committee Meetings and other political working groups are also usually available, unless they concern a matter of national security. Relevant government publications, such as White and Green Papers, departmental reports and press releases

- Journals and press releases published by the European Commission or Parliament

- Party political speeches, manifestos and reports

- Reports by think tanks, research groups, political and pressure groups and economists and academics

- Political media monitoring – the political editors of the BBC, the Daily and Sunday broadsheets and the regional Dailies are respected commentators and have their fingers on the pulse in terms of the main political issues. So too do the editors and correspondents of the best specialist trade journals and magazines. You can undertake media monitoring yourself or sub contract to a specialist monitoring service, many of which are now online

- All relevant websites.

Analysis

Interpretation and analysis should proceed from audit. You will need to identify the real problems and opportunities in a political context. This will lead onto an analysis of the issues for the organisation itself. Is this a proactive expansion or a reactive defence campaign? Do we need to educate opinion formers so that they understand the reality of the situation? How will new policies affect us, our competitors, our customers or suppliers? Are we looking for change in legislation or regulation? Is there a need for an industry-wide response? If so, it may be appropriate for the trade association to take the lead. Or we may decide to act now and on our own.

This is where political experience and knowledge comes into its own. A public affairs specialist can help you with objective advice based on the information collected and can counsel you on the best course of action to take, given the prevailing conditions.

Action

This may take the form of a long-term campaign, with a specific objective in mind, or a very fast response to a 'moving target' crisis. For example, the outbreak of foot and mouth disease required an immediate response from the Farmers Union, the Ramblers Association, food retailers, hoteliers, publicans and others. In either case action must be highly targeted and appropriate for these sensitive audiences. It is generally agreed that the major reasons why public affairs campaigns fail are because they are ill-timed or poorly targeted and do not take into account the lengthy administrative processes and protocols that are a fact of life in politics.

Political targets and ways to reach them

It is a good idea to make friends with your constituency MP/MPs as a matter of course and not simply when you are in trouble or when an issue goes live. Make sure your local MP is briefed about your organisation, is invited to functions when appropriate and knows who you are and what you do. Ideally he or she should be on side and ready to give you support when necessary. A contact of mine fondly nicknamed his constituency MP 'FM' ('she's our 'Friendly Member', she's on our wavelength and she's listened to').

Of course your 'FM' represents your workforce too. If you are a local employer, be aware that, should an industrial dispute take place, your constituency MP has a duty to listen to both sides of the argument. However it is also his/her duty to represent you in parliament and he, she or they – if you have more than one site – should be an early port of call in any public affairs campaign addressing a particular issue.

Your 'FM' can also be very helpful in terms of giving you advice about taking your message out more broadly, particularly if you would like to hold a meeting or reception in a room at the Palace of Westminster, where an MP or peer sponsor is required. Needless to say, your 'FM' should be given a written brief. Similarly if your 'FM' agrees to speak for you, make life as easy as possible for him/her and offer to write a speech or at least to provide bullet points. Always as a matter of courtesy write to thank your 'FM' if he or she speaks on your behalf but refrain from sending gifts so you do not compromise him/her in any way.

Other key targets are MPs who have a particular interest in your organisation or issue. MPs and peers often have established links with particular industries and sectors, especially if they were involved in those sectors before they entered politics. They may also have a personal interest, for example in transport, the arts, women's issues or childcare, education or training, disability or health. This special interest may be expressed by their joining an all party group or association. These groups meet regularly for updates and to provide a forum for discussion and networking. They are prepared to receive presentations from and to meet with representatives from relevant organisations, especially from trade associations. In some instances the group may even agree to receive support from a trade association or cooperative, for example with the provision of secretariat services. It is well worth getting involved with these groups. It might even be possible to create enough interest, championed by one or two particularly empathetic MPs, to start a new one if one does not currently exist covering your particular area.

Civil servants are on the whole friendly and willing to give advice. Senior civil servants are responsible for formulating new policies or drafting bills. They welcome input and reactions from the people who will be most affected by legislation. It is worthwhile cultivating and nurturing contacts in the Department of State relevant to your organisation at whatever level.

Information about constituency MPs, peers, special interest groups and civil servants is freely available and is updated after elections. Good information sources are: Dod's *Parliamentary Companion, Who's Who, Civil Service Yearbook, Vacher's, The Times Guide to the House of Commons*, the *Municipal Yearbook*, the *PMS guide* and Government websites.

When you do communicate with MPs and civil servants, make sure written material or oral briefs are straightforward and to the point. Avoid using corporate jargon or technical language. Don't make communications overtly commercial – you need a public policy angle. Make you aims and objectives clear.

Politics and political processes

The four main things you need to know

1. Depending on your point of view, politics and political processes can be endlessly absorbing or downright dull. Personally, I find politics hugely fascinating and political processes deeply boring. Electorate boredom and apathy were both cited as reasons for the poor turnout at the 2001 General Election.

2. The political party in power and individual MPs will have sets of beliefs about your industry, sector and organisation based on a mixture of fact and prejudice. You may be lucky enough to be flavour of the month, especially if you are generating profits, creating jobs and improving the environment. Conversely you may be unlucky enough to be a pariah if you have a poor reputation or have dubious or unethical practices. Perhaps the most interesting place to be is an unknown quantity where you may simply not have come to their attention, in which case you have the opportunity to get yourself on the map and build a positive profile.

3. We are a lucky enough to live in a democracy – so both you and your organisation are entitled to have political views and to express them freely (the art of public affairs is to express the views sensitively, appropriately and persuasively).

4. Most lobbying nowadays has little to do with bills – because you can't really influence them except perhaps occasionally in non-party controversial areas.

Using a public affairs consultancy

A niche public affairs consultancy or a practice group in one of the larger public relations consultancies can offer much needed specialist advice and objective support in public relations campaign planning and strategy development. In my view, public affairs consultants can offer tremendous value for money. They will interrogate your situation and help you agree a strategic approach. They will guide you though rules and regulations. They will identify the key named targets, help you craft your approach and monitor opinion. If your organisation faces a complex or difficult political situation that needs sensitive handling and you do not have in-house specialist experience or knowledge, then don't try to do it on your own – call in a consultant with the right credentials.

However I would urge caution in terms of profiling when it comes to execution of tactics. By this I mean that it is vital that communications with opinion formers – whether spoken, written or face-to-face – are fronted by *your* people from *your* organisation. It is vital that you take responsibility for this and that you are seen to be responsible for and genuine in the presentation of your case.

Checklist

Public affairs campaign planning

 Do we need to take a planned approach to public affairs?

– Audit issues

– Analysis

 Is the current administration broadly supportive of or hostile towards our organisation? Do we have any particular supporters or critics?

– Audit opinions

– Analysis

 Do we have effective monitoring?

– Reports

– Media monitoring

– Online monitoring

 Do we have up-to-date research?

– Polls and public opinion

 What are our objectives?

– Legislative or regulatory introduction/reform/ relaxation? Awareness?

chapter thirteen

Event management

Introduction

Face-to-face events with a public relations purpose and linked to other marketing activities can be powerful channels to deliver important and sometimes complex messages to key target audiences, helping to build reputation in a very up close and personal way. This is the right forum to communicate the importance of an issue, to give new information, to project the values and stature of the organisation, to demonstrate how the organisation respects and values the views and opinions of the invited target audience.

But, in terms of the frenetic way we live our lives, is there still a role for face-to-face communication? People are now busier than ever before and every time management course preaches the need to prioritise – is this event really one I need to attend? New technology is enabling us to have one-to-one communication with individuals without the need to shake hands, share a drink or move from the comfort of our offices or homes.

Evidence suggests that there is in fact a growing desire for face-to-face meeting in preference to other forms of communication. Research published by the Consumer Association in 2001 said that the number of people preferring face-to-face meetings as their preferred way of communicating had increased from 39% to 67% over the previous twelve months. The novelty of electronic communications has waned somewhat. People are beginning to realise that e-communication serves a different function. People will go to events – and in great numbers – providing it is clear what's in it for them, that logistics are attendee-friendly and that invitees have enough notice to get themselves organised to be there. Human beings will always need contact and, as less contact takes place on a day-to-day basis, so relevant, appropriate and tailored face-to-face events become even more important as a way of keeping in touch.

Whether you are organising a round table discussion for ten or twelve business gurus, an advisory panel meeting for a group of the country's top neurologists or a public meeting to discuss a local planning appli-cation, the central principles remain the same. However, unless you have particular expertise or have your own special events team in-house, do consider using a special event organiser. Their extensive experience will help ensure that your event runs smoothly. Indeed when you are putting together your PR strategy an initial consultancy session with a special events organiser may give you new and creative ideas about how the inclusion of appropriately designed events might deliver considerable added value to your PR programme.

Types of events

Conferences and exhibitions

Designed to bring a large number of people together to discuss common issues. Associations and unions may also bolt on an annual general meeting for members and use the exhibition facilities to generate income. The event may be sponsored – and therefore owned – by your organisation or it may be an event where your organisation is playing a subsidiary role, with, say, a stand or exhibit, the sponsorship of a fringe meeting or taking up a speaking platform. If it is owned by your organisation, this is probably the most complex event scenario and one where an event/conference management company should be called in as soon as possible. There may be an overt sales objective or the main aim may be to reach a large number of individuals, representing an important target market, to build bridges, to gain opinions and undertake research or to reassure after a difficult period.

Sales conferences

Designed to motivate the frontline sales team. They usually include performance data and encourage competition between sales teams. They are often used as briefing meetings to tell teams about new products and services that they will be expected to sell and may unveil new advertising etc. They may also include training sessions on sales or customer service. They may be residential if the sales team work from home. PRs are sometimes asked to help organise part or all of these events.

Internal staff events and briefings etc.

Designed for internal communications purposes, sometimes one offs, sometimes as part of a change management programme, sometimes regular, routine events that happen quarterly/annually. They may be held on- or off-site. Obviously there is far more control of on-site events – quite apart from the fact that they are usually cheaper. They may involve large numbers of people or smaller groups and may be phased over a period of time to get to all staff over a region or over the country.

Satellite conferences and debates

At its simplest video conferencing, at its most sophisticated a multi-site entertainment extravaganza for a private audience, with the look and feel of a TV show. Used when it is judged to be impossible to bring opinion formers and influencers from all over the country together – for example doctors or Business Link advisers – or when people are based in several different countries. They can also be used as part of internal communications programmes for international companies. Local events are organised for groups, often in TV studios, which are linked up. The end result looks like a linked series of outside broadcasts facilitating debate and discussion across sites. They are very effective in terms of surrounding the organisation with positive associations as a facilitator and for establishing clout and importance in a sector.

Awards ceremonies

The culmination of a project that involves a competition or a nomination/voting system, involving peers (like the Oscars), fans (like the Brit Awards) or specific groups with a vested interest (like parents, invited to vote for their Teacher of the Year). There are thousands of awards ceremonies every year and these are often in specific industry sectors, associated with or sponsored by media – often the main industry trade press title, for example *What Car's* Car of the Year Awards or, in our own industry, the *PR Week* Awards. Awards ceremonies can surround an organisation with a 'warm glow' and can help drive awareness of a brand name (Booker Prize) or an issue (National Training Awards). Pre-publicity is vital. Television coverage may even be possible, as part of a sponsorship package. Event logistics may be complicated particularly if there is to be complex staging, music and lighting – a prime example of when an events management company should be called in.

Seminars and workshops

Theses have many purposes and can be tailored to suit many target audiences, from graduates entering a profession to experienced people who want to sharpen their practice or skills set. Because they involve smaller numbers than a lecture, the cost per head will be higher. However the opportunity to drive key messages home in-depth – and to perhaps achieve a change in perception or behaviour – is greater. These sorts of events also enable you to recruit ambassadors to perhaps act as advocates for your organisation and to speak with knowledge and experience – people who understand you and the sector you operate in and the specific issues facing your sector.

Private breakfasts, lunches or dinners

Used to gain information from and to network with selected individuals. Only suitable for small groups where the interests are shared and where the tone is informal and intimate. A prestigious boardroom occasion for eight to twelve VIPs including an important guest of honour, sector guru or respected speaker can work well to attract important targets and to create a powerful forum for discussion and debate.

Lectures

Designed to bring together opinion formers and influencers and packaged so that the organisation is surrounded with positive values and kudos. Suitable not only for organisations with a serious academic or research based orientation but also for professional organisations where theory can be brought alive and even made sexy via a controversial, whizzy and entertaining presentation. It may be a launch platform for a new report or paper and it can be treated as an opportunity for networking, which may be followed by a drinks party and canapés. It may be used to offer exclusive media relations' opportunities to highly desirable media targets.

Press conferences and photocalls

For example, on site after a rail crash or to announce the launch of a new drug that will reduce deaths from cancer, or featuring a celebrity supporter. Only consider a press conference if the news you have to deliver is really strong, the issue your organisation is involved with is in the headlines or you have an A-list celebrity supporter. I have tackled both press conferences and photocalls as separate issues in chapter eight.

Parties

Which may be to celebrate a launch of a new perfume, to mark a significant anniversary for an organisation, to open a new restaurant, to kick off or conclude a sponsored exhibition, sports event, concert or festival. If the story is really newsworthy or has an amusing or quirky angle, the more you increase the chances of achieving media coverage. An A-list celebrity attendance might tip the balance, but don't bank on it.

Ten rules for event management

1. Use your common sense and don't underestimate how much planning and organisational time is needed.

2. Get the venue first – provisionally book three if you must but do this first.

3. Give people plenty of notice – send out dates for diaries four to six months or even a year ahead if you want top flight people – follow up with invites.

4. Brief staff on duty carefully – on the day these people are your organisation's ambassadors.

5. If you are including breakout sessions and workshops build in time for people movement.

6. If you can, make it a weekend event as hotels and conference centres are less busy and may be willing to negotiate on price.

7. Invite guests' partners too for a better attendance level.

8. If there any more than 40 guests consider sub-contracting to an event management consultancy – delegate properly and let the event management company liaise with the venue etc.

9. Make events interactive and participative – people like to express opinions and to have a chance to share ideas rather than be lectured at.

10. Treat every one you have invited as an individual.

Checklist

Planning

✓ Has this been done before? Do we have any benchmarks? Did we achieve our objectives? If not, why not? How can we improve?

✓ What are our objectives for *this* event?

✓ What type(s) of audience(s) and how many are we targeting?

✓ How do we make this event attractive to and relevant to them? How can we make it a 'must attend' occasion?
  – Location and ease of travel
  – Date and time
  – Content
  – Partners?

✓ Content – what do we need to include?
  – Speakers
  – Celebrities and/or chairperson
  – AV
  – Display
  – Give aways/delegate packs/papers/digests/event 'newspaper' etc.
  – Competitions.

✓ Are there any networking opportunities?

✓ Critical path – up to the event and including any follow-up.

✓ How much will the event cost, in total and broken
down by:

- Set, stands and/or displays – space costs,
  design and build, equipment, transportation and
  storage, samples, prizes, give aways and gifts,
  branded merchandise

- Supporting hospitality and complementary
  events – e.g. press reception, business briefing,
  private drinks party, sponsored dinner – venue
  hire, catering, speakers, entertainment,
  set/branded backdrop

- Print – all materials e.g. packs, leaflets,
  invitations, etc.

- Staffing – fees, accommodation, catering, travel,
  celebrity/speaker fees if required

- Marketing – advertising, leafleting

- Sponsorship.

Action

✓ Delegate guest management – invitations, RSVP
monitoring, joining instructions, accommodation,
management on the day, including stewarding,
goodie bags, gifts and give aways.

✓ VIP speaker management – speakers' briefing and
support, chairman's notes, breakout session format.

✓ Event management – booking, liaison with venue,
recce, access, room layouts, set/stand design
and build, set-up, set strike and get out, print
materials, catering.

✓ Staff management – hire additional staff, staff briefing, transport and accommodation, corporate clothing/dress code.

✓ Media relations – media invitation and press desk/press office management, at exhibitions and conferences, press day attendance.

✓ Support materials – literature, brochure/catalogue copy, advertising.

Evaluation

✓ Review meeting as soon after the event as is practicable.

✓ What went well and what could have worked better?

✓ Write summary report so that lessons learnt are captured for next time.

✓ Circulate report to management and anyone who has an interest in the event.

chapter fourteen

International public relations

Introduction

Many PR professionals working in-house are now involved with international public relations to a greater or lesser extent. Your organisation may be a major international plc, with operational bases in many countries. You may be a UK company with interests all over the world. You may have just one or two specific export markets in Europe, North America or the Far East. Whatever your current situation, it is highly likely that, at some stage in your career, you will be involved in international public relations.

With more and more mergers and acquisitions, PR practitioners working in consultancy are now often part of major international networks, offering international programme co-ordination and/or implementation to clients, working as part of a team with colleagues they may never have met, in Singapore and Moscow, Lisbon and Melbourne. Likewise there may be times when you find yourself working for a client based outside the UK who needs PR support in the UK, even reporting to another consultancy, appointed to handle programme coordination. These situations require additional and different skills, compared to traditional PR.

Handling the media for international campaigns is also very different today from the way it was a few years ago. We communicate instantly via the Internet and e-mail with both colleagues and journalists across the globe, regardless of the time zone or political territory. English dominates as the worldwide business language, the ubiquitous language of the Internet and the cross-border language of the media. Journalists and photographers, and cameramen and sound recordists transmit copy, sound and visuals instantly from London to New York, from Rome to Tokyo for Internet news broadcast, terrestrial and cable TV, for the national dailies, for radio. If you really want to you can download the latest headlines off the Internet on your mobile phone while trekking across the Gobi Desert.

International public relations is an expensive business if you want to do it well and get it right. There are few economies of scale – even if you develop a central strategy, it is acknowledged that PR programmes must be tailored to suit the local market conditions. Perhaps the only exception is the central development of your web presence, which can be accessed by anyone and everyone, anywhere in the world. But even then you need localised versions, written in the vernacular for each country you operate in.

The big issues are how do you plan and manage PR international programmes in this brave new world of instant communications and distant teams? What should be your objectives? How do you formulate a workable international strategy? Who takes central and local responsibility for the programme management and execution? Do you impose the creative strategy from the centre or allow for local variation? What resources do you need to make it happen and how do you know if the programme is meeting its objectives?

Definition

International public relations – a public relations plan and programme which is executed in more than one language or is managed in more than two countries.

International PR management

Like any team activity, it is relatively easy to manage a PR programme which involves just two parties. The simplest international programmes are usually hatched in the organisation's area of origin and involve just one other area. When organisations start to expand, the first move is usually to enter a new market that is geographically close, or one that has similar social, economic or business ethics and values.

Management becomes more complex when more parties, more countries, more cultures and more languages are involved. Whether you are working with a colleague in the same organisation, a client or a local consultancy, you will need to be crystal clear about relationships, responsibilities and who the ultimate decision maker is. Positive internal communications policies are vital particularly if you are going to avoid the 'not invented here' syndrome.

If travel and accommodation can be afforded, a face-to-face meeting is by far the best way to kick off an international programme, where everyone involved can get together, get to know and feel comfortable with each other and thrash out ways of working effectively as a team, albeit in many different locations. Video conferencing is a possible alternative but is usually less effective in terms of establishing strong working relationships that survive misunderstandings and remain cohesive if the going gets tough.

Regular communication by phone and e-mail is naturally vital to keep all parties up-to-date with progress or problems and to encourage a strong sense of teamwork. Some teams use news bulletins, delivered electronically, as a way of keeping in touch. If the programme is going to be a continuous one or a PR consultant is likely to work on more international campaigns in the future, foreign language courses can be a great way to improve individual skills and confidence in international negotiations.

The significance of the web

The power and influence of the web is central to successful international public relations. You must have a fully functional, regularly updated website. It may need to be updated every day – even hourly – if you are working in a big corporate or fast moving sector. It should have a dedicated press office area, controlled centrally with country-by-country references or pages as required. Forget initial phone calls, this is where people who are interested in your organisation head for first – journalists, analysts, students, Joe Public. The website is your window to the world. Make sure it reflects your corporate values and communicates your corporate messages and that it is easy to navigate – design it so that it meets the needs of the media.

International PR planning

This is much the same as any other PR planning. You need to work through the steps in the same way, reviewing the different influences and prevailing conditions in each country where you plan to operate a PR programme.

However, before you embark on the planning process, you do need to organise yourself and make some important decisions:

- **Strategic direction** – is there a clear statement about the organisation and its aims and objectives, as far as the PR strategy is concerned?

- **Human resources** – will the programme be planned, managed and executed in-house or will one or more consultancies be used? Do you have a strong internal PR group and network, with the right people in each country to do the job that needs doing? Do you need to train local people to do the job? Who will direct? Who will coordinate, manage and execute? If you need to select and recruit consultancies, what criteria will be used and how will the search be conducted? Is one international consultancy group preferable to locally selected consultancies? Do we need specialist consultancies (e.g. healthcare, financial)?

- **Legal aspects** – if consultancies are hired, what contracts will be entered into? What duration should they cover? What notice period and exclusion criteria? Is the consultancy prohibited from handling competitive business in territories not currently involved? Would existing arrangements with competitors in one or more countries have to be terminated?

- **Financial resources and budgeting** – How will this be handled? Will all the accounting be done in euros or US dollars? Is there provision for currency fluctuation in any contracts with consultancies? Are there effective financial management systems in place? Is there a separate budget for coordination? If using consultancies, is there a contingency built in for over-servicing? (This is particularly important if this is the first time an international programme is being conducted and there is no benchmark.)

- **Evaluation and reporting systems** – what systems do you need to set up to meet your needs?

Central v local

- The best way to avoid the 'not invented here' syndrome is to consult and seek buy-in to the programme from the many individuals who will be involved in its delivery. It will take time and patience.

- Once a basic brief is written, collect views and ideas.

- Circulate the first draft plan and programme to those who will be responsible for it and allow them to adapt and modify the programme for the local markets.

- Establish policies or sets of rules, outlining what must remain common in every location (corporate identity, core messages, programme theme, document templates, facts and figures including financial information, frequently asked questions and answers etc.).

- Local tactics and logistics may need major or minor modification – listen to your local people and act on their advice.

The role of the coordinator

The coordinator of an international campaign plays many roles.

Diplomat

Running international business can feel like working at the Foreign Office or being an ambassador – and you are sometimes treated in the same way! The good coordinator handles problems with grace and charm and smoothes ruffled feathers when necessary.

Policeman

On the other hand the good coordinator is also tough and knows when the rules have been broken and takes action to prevent it happening again.

Translator

Even though English is the acknowledged business language all over the world there will be times when misunderstandings happen, as a result of idiomatic expression or misunderstood terminology – the good coordinator is aware of this, develops an eye and ear for misunderstanding and clarifies using simple vocabulary.

Librarian

The good coordinator is organised and tidy so that even if he/she is not in the office, papers can be located and invoices traced. The more countries that are involved, the more organised the coordinator needs to be.

Communicator

The good coordinator knows that people are more motivated, respond better and work together if they understand why they are doing what they are doing. He/she looks for opportunities to communicate and puts in place systems and channels which facilitate good communication.

Chameleon

The good coordinator will make subtle changes to the way he/she behaves when working with different people from different cultures in order to make them feel at ease and to elicit a favourable response/outcome.

Circus artist

9am – an e-mail from Jakarta asking for new corporate photography – midday a phone call asking for the corporate line to a crisis that has just happened in Cape Town – 8pm a call on the mobile from an irate Chief Executive who wants to know why his photo didn't appear in the *New York Times* – the good coordinator needs to be able to juggle a hundred and one issues, will sometimes walk the tightrope and may have to tame a few wild animals too!

Budgeting and billing

As I mentioned above, international PR does not come cheap. When planning a budget, make sure you include all the usual things but additionally build in a few extra considerations:

- **Fees** – differ markedly from country to country, at the time of writing lower in Italy and Germany than in the UK. You need to budget country by country based on local market conditions

- **Ways of working** – in order to manage international PR programmes, some organisations set a capped monthly or quarterly fee. This seems sensible to control costs, however some flexibility in the form of a contingency should be built in so that opportunities can be taken and issues can be dealt with

- **Time for and costs of travel** – negotiate corporate rates with a travel and hotel booking company

- **Subsistence and expenses** – especially if people are spending long stretches abroad

- **Exchange rates** – unless you are working in one currency, rates will fluctuate – be clear about billing dates and what rates should apply

- **Invoicing systems** – if you are responsible for coordination, devise a sensible invoicing system and bully people into getting invoices to you on time.

Agency and interagency relationships

While strategies may be devised centrally and cascaded through the network, it is crucial that the people on the ground work well together. Local consultancies must develop good working relationships with local clients as well as colleagues and clients at the centre.

If a network is created using different consultancies in different locations, reporting into yet another coordinating consultancy, try to bury the competitive hatchet. This is no time for turf wars. There will be occasions when things go wrong but if another consultancy performs badly, don't use the opportunity to stab people in the back. If there are problems, try to sort them out – work for the common good and for the benefit of the corporate reputation. If you can't resolve an issue, take proper action but don't resort to bitching about other PR practitioners – it simply isn't professional.

Language and cultural differences

This subject is worth a hefty book in its own right.

While English is the recognised universal business language and many business people across the world have some grasp of English, there is plenty of room for misunderstanding and confusion. Don't make any assumptions and check people understand what you are saying or writing. Don't use jargon and explain complex concepts using plain English and simple vocabulary. Idioms, metaphors and similes pose the most frequent problems. Watch out for obscurity.

It is tempting to fall back to stereotypes – the Northern European with the Presbyterian work ethic, the Southern European who likes a siesta, the Oriental who always says 'yes' in order to save 'face', the 'shoot from the hip' American. There are of course real cultural differences, particularly in terms of social customs and these can pose some difficulties. Check out the most important customs and issues for each country you work with or in. Make sure you cause no offence, whether through the production of materials for the public relations campaign or as a result of the behaviour of your people working in or visiting another country.

I once directed a European campaign for an Iranian company which involved taking a party of German, British, French, Spanish and Italian journalists and photographers on a press trip to Tehran and southern Iran. As you would imagine it was quite a challenge getting such a mixed group to work together in a country with such a different cultural backdrop. Moreover we had to create a campaign with a central theme rolled out to each of the countries, including Iran. Our Iranian hosts were charming, even the security men who followed us were quietly polite and the government ministers we met were welcoming and interested in what we were doing. More importantly the work we were able to do and the media coverage we achieved was excellent. The main lessons I learnt were:

• Follow the rules – it is impolite and inappropriate to challenge the regime of any country especially if you are working there and are in effect a guest. If there is a dress code, adhere to it. If women need to behave differently to the way they behave at home, so be it. If alcohol consumption is frowned upon, leave it out and always respect religious custom.

• Ask clients, colleagues or hosts for advice about what is and what is not acceptable and how to behave.

- Buy a guide book about the country you are working with or in – *Lonely Planet* and *Rough Guides* are especially good on cultural differences.

- Don't make assumptions.

- Learn to say 'Thank you', 'Pleased to meet you' and 'I have enjoyed working with you' in the local language.

Creative strategies in international campaigns

If you are or want to be an internationally recognised brand name it is important to try to achieve some sort of consistency in your communication programme, as more and more target audiences move across national and international boundaries. It has been done by advertisers for decades.

It is possible to formulate a coherent creative strategy providing it is capable of translation in each local country, even if it is simply through the use of different tactics. For example one of the EC Olive Oil campaigns I directed had the creative theme 'Olive Oil – the Taste for Life' – which meant we could talk about learning to use olive oil (developing a taste for it), the many different tastes of olive oils (varying from light sweet Provencal oils to chunky robust oils from Lerida in Spain), through to its role in a healthy diet (which means you enjoy life to the full and ultimately may even enjoy a longer life). We used consistently strong graphics in leaflets, advertising, exhibition stands and so on, majoring on Mediterranean foods. This campaign theme could have been used in any country in the world. Good strong creative strategies also help teams in many different locations to feel part of a greater whole.

International media

You need to manage expectations and educate clients accordingly, as the media scene is quite different in different countries. The most important difference is that the UK has the most powerful national daily press corp in the world. Most other countries' media is based round regional and local press. And while it might be normal to get 45 journalists along to a press briefing in Italy, that would be incredibly unusual here in the UK. Maybe the media here is just too wised up to public relations? Maybe more people work in the media in other countries round the world so there are more journalists able to go out of the office to briefings? Maybe overseas journalists will always make time for a press briefing with a decent lunch and a little siesta to follow?

Contracts

As in any business situation, you must agree and sign a legally binding contract with every partner and supplier you work with, for every country you work in. You will need to take advice about whether or not the law of the relevant country must apply or whether you can write the contract under English law. Never rely on 'gentleman's contracts'.

Getting started

Where are you now? Where do you need to be?

Situation	Cost	Solution(s)
Can't afford full-blown international PR but must make a start	£	• Concentrate on the website, a really good interactive online press office and 24/7 contact numbers
Need to build media contacts country by country but have no in-house infrastructure and can't afford a PR consultancy	££	• Take out your main spokesperson/people on a roadshow – a series of face-to-face interviews with main media in each country you have an interest in • Cultivate a key journalist in each country you are interested in and invite each one for an individual 'getting to know you' session – bring him/her to the base for a site visit, briefing and – build in some relaxation and tourist time – a visit to a new gallery, a new restaurant, a new musical • Establish contacts with foreign correspondents based in the UK (mainly in London, with a few in Edinburgh) • Use international news agencies like UNS who will put out news for you (for a fee) • Investigate the services offered by news agencies that work by language (i.e. Reuters is English, AFP is French, DPA is German) • Some organisations still use direct mailings of newsletters and bulletins to overseas contacts – using a central design template with local adaptation into local language – however the web is more cost-effective

Have to co-ordinate the in-house operational PR practitioners in every country	£££	• Review internal communications systems and set up an intranet system • Have regular get-togethers, based on need • Compile regular monthly reports, quarterly summaries and annual reviews • Agree budget management system • Agree central and local responsibilities including strategy development

Need to appoint PR consultancies in each country/ PR consultancy with its own network	£££	• Select either:
		    – Consultancy network
		    – Local suppliers
		
		• Work through pitch process outlined in chapter eight.

Checklist

✓ Allocate adequate budgets and insist on tight financial systems.

✓ Make sure your Internet site meets the needs of your international community, especially journalists.

✓ Agree a strategy for how international public relations will be managed and coordinated.

✓ Agree on parameters for local tailoring.

✓ Appoint a skilled coordinator – he or she may not be a PR professional but should have administrative and communication skills.

✓ Create a network and ensure the network communicates well using new technology.

✓ Invest in network meetings – if not quarterly then at least annually. Nothing beats a face-to-face meeting for ironing out communication difficulties.

✓ Respect social conventions in the countries in which you operate.

✓ Consider language lessons.

chapter fifteen

Public relations, new media and technology

Introduction

New media and its effect on target audiences

Using new media to enhance reputation

Harnessing new technology in PR practice

Checklist

Introduction

I have met a few crusty old PR professionals, clients and colleagues who, even now, remain unenthusiastic about new developments in communications:

- *'The definition of public relations hasn't changed with the arrival of new media and the Internet'*

- *'New media is hyped out of all proportion'*

- *'New media hasn't had much impact on me and I'm pretty typical'*

- *'I don't want a PC on my desk and I don't use e-mail or the Internet – my secretary does all that'*

- *'Journalists don't like new media'*

- *'How on earth can we expect to understand the complexities or keep up with the pace of change? We must stick with tried and tested techniques and leave new media and the Internet to the advertising agencies and specialists'*

These are all more or less verbatim quotes.

By 2005 commentators predict that 70%+ of homes and 95% of businesses will be Internet connected. Most businesses – even the smallest SME – now consider a website as a 'must have' marketing tool, a hygiene factor, no longer simply an add-on, indeed for many *the* starting point for communication. We increasingly use websites as shop windows and as the preferred places to pick up information about and then go on to buy products and services. Intranets play a vital role in internal communications. Extranets keep suppliers and partners in the communication loop. Satellite and cable broadcasting is fragmenting audiences and changing the way people view, listen and behave.

New entrants into the PR profession have grown up and are entirely familiar with these new concepts and new ways of thinking. The distinction between old and new is almost slipping away. New media is no longer new and arguably should now be considered simply as **more** media communication via other channels.

New technology is working towards convergence. The multipurpose flat screen TV/hi-fi/radio/Internet-connected PC/video phone is no longer a sci-fi fiction, it's a practical fact and will probably be affordable for most householders by 2015.

Some PR practitioners are completely fascinated by new media and want to become experts in the subject. Some remain so intimidated by it that they prefer to leave it to specialist consultancies or more enthusiastic colleagues. But as far as most PR practitioners are concerned, there are three key questions that need to be asked when planning a PR campaign:

1. Is/are my target audience(s) affected and influenced by new media/the Internet/technology? How are they using it?

2. Can I use new media/the Internet/technology to enhance my organisation's reputation among the target audience(s)?

3. How can new media/the Internet/technology be harnessed to help me work more cost-effectively?

New media and its effect on target audiences

Advertising and direct marketing professionals were perhaps the first to understand and use new media effectively to reach target audiences. No longer could they simply rely on a few commercial terrestrial TV channels and radio stations to reach the majority of their target audiences.

New media is digital media and has resulted in:

- Expanding choice in traditional media – terrestrial TV channels, radio stations, newspapers and magazines which have launched accompanying websites, many of which carry programming as well as other editorial and advertising

- New satellite and cable TV and radio channels from the UK, mainland Europe and the rest of the world

- Interactive TV – engaging with the target directly and inviting a response in a two-way dialogue.

Using new media to enhance reputation

Use new media just as you do old media – as a channel to your target. Your website enables you to get news out quickly, reactively as a channel to issue rebuttals and proactively to get good news out as quickly as you can to your main targets. Using new media no longer means you are cutting edge – it simply indicates you are catching up with the early adopters. But use new media subtly, not like a sledgehammer. Don't be tempted to send unsolicited e-mails or text messages to the media. In fact indiscriminate use of new media could serve to damage your reputation rather than enhance it, particularly with the media.

Harnessing new technology in PR practice

PR is a 24/7 job. The media is working round the clock and your availability is vital especially when managing an issue or crisis. It can also make all the difference between making the most of a media opportunity and letting it slip out of your hands. Small, powerful, multifunctional and getting cheaper all the time – the newest developments in technology deliver added value in terms of managing the PR function effectively and efficiently. While your budget will inevitably dictate what you can afford, this is the wish list of the most useful tools on the market at the time of writing.

Technology	How it helps
E-mail	When was the last time someone told you they didn't have e-mail? Instant access to all areas, from Aylesbury to Zanzibar, e-mail has become the most vital and fastest written communication tool. Increasing numbers of journalists want press releases as e-mails. Attachments are irritating if they can't be opened first time so you may have to forsake the beautifully designed press paper/ letterhead in order to make it easy for the journalist. And avoid the release being sent to the recycle bin just because it can't be opened. Check your contacts aren't phobic that you are peddling viruses. Some journalists have been known to bin e-mails if there is any suspicion about their origin.

Technology	How it helps
Fax	Old fashioned stalwart.
Internet access	Again a vital communications tool. As a PR practitioner you should have some input into your organisation's website. At the very least you should have an online press office where latest press releases are posted and where journalists can get basic facts. The Internet is also a fantastic research tool, especially when you are planning campaigns, auditing the marketplace and checking out competitive activity. And of course it is a time saver for business people, whether you are looking for travel information, want to make a booking or are ordering office supplies.
Pager	Nifty gadgets if you don't need/want a mobile phone or want to equip a number of personnel staffing a press office cost effectively. Slip one into a handbag or jacket pocket.
Mobile phone – WAP enabled	Given the fact that 24/7 is the rule rather than the exception in PR, most practitioners are now equipped with a mobile phone – either issued by the office or because they have taken personal responsibility to make sure they are contactable. A mobile number is often included in press releases especially if the release is going out on a Friday or over a holiday period. The latest mobile phones do almost everything a PC can, from sending e-mails to connecting to the Internet.
Answerphone	At home as well as at the office for out-of-hours calls and to buy time – screen media calls so that you can call back when you have had a chance to consider what response you need to make or to contact colleagues or consultants.

Technology	How it helps
Voicemail	Again a pretty common feature in most organisations today. Some PR consultancies believe that voicemail isn't appropriate if a quality service is offered to a client, and clients should be able to talk to someone immediately at any time. On the other hand some clients are happy with voicemail providing calls are returned within a specified time – occasionally this is stipulated as a key performance indicator.
Hands free phone	Really useful and prevents neck ache and bad posture if you are referring to proofs and need both hands or a colleague needs to hear the call too – in other words a rudimentary conference call. If you are responsible for the press office and find yourself on the phone for long stretches or are running an emergency press office which will take a large volume of calls in a short time, it might also be worthwhile investing in a headset.
Stored numbers and voice activated dialling	One step up from short code dialling. If you have a defined number of people – media or clients – who you call very frequently, voice activation may save a little time.
Call forwarding	Useful if you are in a remote location but want a seamless connection with media, clients and colleagues – your usual phone forwards calls to another phone. Your caller thinks you are in your usual location when in fact you are 200 miles away.
Laptops, palmtops and electronic notepads and organisers	Again many people would consider one of these to be an absolute basic that no practitioner can do without. Vital for the press office on the move, working in hotel rooms, sending e-releases via the Internet from any location – remember the mains adaptor if working abroad. Some have built-in printers and all are now Internet ready. Not all can do everything – yet – but in the not too distant future you can expect convergence so these items will be capable of telephony too. Eventually you'll need just one piece of kit – in the size to suit your way of working – or your eyesight!

Technology	How it helps
Digital projector	A basic for presentations in most businesses, particularly used by consultancies when pitching for business. However, some practitioners consider this an overused format and have reverted to old-fashioned overheads or just a fabulous performance without any technological distraction.
Scanners	Photocopiers for the 21st century that enable you to manipulate pictures and copy and cut down copy typing, for example when updating old literature and manuals created before PCs were commonplace and information was digitalised.
ASR (Automatic Speech Recognition)	Train your PC to take dictation – it is more efficient than asking a PA to transcribe a tape and you can edit and use electronic data immediately to create releases and copy. It hasn't replaced touch-typing – yet – but it will increasingly be offered as part of the software kit built into PC packages.

Checklist

✓ Invest in the latest technology.

✓ Equip your team with the right kit so they can work efficiently and effectively.

✓ Make sure the website is working as hard as it can.

✓ Use the web for research and ideas.

✓ Understand how your target audiences are using new technology and media and adapt plans accordingly.

✓ Read one new media trade press title regularly.

✓ Don't be a slave to technology – you are the communicator, technology merely offers new channels to deliver your message.

✓ Consider low-tech presentations for a change – most people in business are weary of PowerPoint presentations.

✓ Turn off or mute your mobile phone whenever you can – particularly in public spaces.

appendices

Appendix 1: Selected bibliography

The IPR Toolkit

Michael Fairchild MIPR

The Institute of Public Relations (IPR)

Definitive industry handbook on planning research and evaluation, propagating recognised and common standards – updated summer 2001.

Essentials of Marketing

Jim Blythe

Financial Times Pitman Publishing

Comprehensive look at marketing, full of models and concepts.

Marketing: Concepts and Strategies

Dibb, Simkin, Pride and Ferrell

Pitman Publishing

Useful round up for PR practitioners working in a marketing environment.

The Globalisation of Business

John Dunning

Routledge

A bit academic but none the less a clear overview.

Essentials of Market Research

Tony Proctor

Pitman Publishing

Useful guide to how to use market research.

British Conference Destinations Directory

British Association of Conference Towns

Free annual directory providing useful information about conference venues across the UK.

BRAD

Maclean Hunter

Invaluable directory giving data on media in the UK.

Conference Green and Blue Books
Benn Business Information Services

Companion volumes giving, in the green volume, conference venues, and in the blue volume, information about capacities, facilities, dimensions etc.

Effective Public Relations
Scott M Cutlip, Allen H Cente, Glan M Brom
Prentice-Hall International Inc

First published in 1952 and into its eighth imprint – an academic tome which is particularly invaluable if you are interested in the history and practice of PR with a heavy US bias.

Exploring Corporate Strategy
Gerry Johnson & Kevan Scholes
Prentice-Hall International Inc

An overview of corporate planning.

Managing The Message
Peter Hobday
London House

Entertaining and highly readable advice on handling the media from one of Britain's best-loved broadcasters.

Public Relations
Frank Jefkin
Pearson Professional

Classic textbook, one of many by the late Frank Jefkin.

The Management and Practice of Public Relations
Norman Stone
Macmillan Business

Good all-round introduction.

Appendix 2: Useful contacts

Advertising Association (AA)

Abford House

15 Wilton Road, London SW1V 1NJ

tel: 020 7828 2771

web: www.adassoc.org.uk

Audit Bureau of Circulations Ltd (ABC)

Saxon House, High Street

Berkhamstead, Herts HP4 1AD

tel: 01442 870800

web: www.abc.org.uk

Broadcasters' Audience Research Board (BARB)

18 Dering Street

London W1R 9AF

tel: 020 7529 5531

web: www. barb.co.uk

Institute of Advertising Practitioners (IPA)

44 Belgrave Square

London SW1X 8QS

tel: 020 7235 7020

web: www.ipa.co.uk

Advertising Standards Authority (ASA)

Brook House, 2-16 Torrington Place

London WC1E 7HN

tel: 020 7580 5555

web: www.asa.org.uk

Broadcast Standards Commission

7 The Sanctuary

London SW1P 3JS

tel: 020 7233 0544

web: www.bsc.org.uk

Association of Media Evaluation Companies

52 Lyford Road

London SW18 3LF

tel: 020 8874 5981

web: www.amec.org.uk

British Broadcasting Company (BBC)
Broadcasting House
London W1A 1AA
tel: 020 8743 8000
web: www.bbc.co.uk

Direct Marketing Association (DMA)
Haymarket House
1 Oxendon Street
London SW1Y 4EE
tel: 020 7321 2525
web: www.dma.org.uk

Independent Television Commission (ITC)
33 Foley Street
London W1P 7LB
tel: 020 7255 3000
web: www.itc.org.uk

Public Relations Consultants Association (PRCA)
Willow House, Willow Place
Victoria, London SW1P 1JH
tel: 020 7233 6026
web: www.prca.org.uk

Institute of Public Relations (IPR)
The Old Trading House
15 Northburgh Street
London EC1V 0PR
tel: 020 7253 5151
web: www.ipr.org.uk

Market Research Society (MRS)
15 Northburgh Street
London EC1V 0AH
tel: 020 7490 4911
web: www.mrs.org.uk

National Readership Surveys (NRS)
42 Drury Lane, Covent Garden
London WC2B 5RT
tel: 020 7632 2915
web: www.nrs.co.uk

Newspaper Publishers Association (NPA)

33 Southwark Bridge Road

London SE1 9EU

tel: 020 7928 6928

web: no website at time of writing

Newspaper Society

Bloomsbury House

74-77 Great Russell Street

London WC1B 3DA

tel: 020 7636 7014

web: www.newspapersoc.org.uk

Periodical Publishers Association

Queen's House

28 Kingsway, London WC2B 6JR

tel: 020 7404 4166

web: www.ppa.co.uk

Radio Authority

Holbrook House

14 Great Queen Street

London WC2B 5DG

tel: 020 7430 2724

web: www.radioauthority.org.uk

Radio Joint Audience Research (RAJAR)

Gainsborough House

81 Oxford Street

London W1D 2EU

tel: 020 7930 5350

web: www.rajar.co.uk

The Media Trust

3-7 Euston Centre, Regent's Place

London NW1 3JG

tel: 020 7874 7600

web: www.mediatrust.org

**The Communication, Advertising
and Marketing Foundation (CAM)**
Moor Hall, Cookham
Maidenhead SL6 9QH
tel: 020 7828 7506
web: www.camfoundation.com

PIMS
Pims House
Mildmay Avenue
London N1 4RS
tel: 020 7354 7020
web: www.pims.co.uk

Hollis Publishing
Harlequin House
7 High Street, Teddington
Middlesex TW11 8EL
tel: 020 8977 7711
web: www.hollis-pr.com

PR Week (Haymarket Publishing)
174 Hammersmith Road
London W6 1JP
tel: 020 8267 4464/4520
web: www.prweek.com

Appendix 3: Codes of Conduct

Reproduced with the permission of the Institute of Public Relations.

IPR Code of Conduct – October 2000 IPR Principles

1. Members of the Institute of Public Relations agree to:

    *   Maintain the highest standards of professional endeavour, integrity, confidentiality, financial propriety and personal conduct;

    *   Deal honestly and fairly in business with employers, employees, clients, fellow professionals, other professions and the public;

    *   Respect the customs, practices and codes of clients, employers, colleagues, fellow professionals and other professions in all countries where they practise;

    *   Take all reasonable care to ensure employment best practice including giving no cause for complaint of unfair discrimination on any grounds;

    *   Work within the legal and regulatory frameworks affecting the practice of public relations in all countries where they practise;

    *   Encourage professional training and development among members of the profession;

    *   Respect and abide by this Code and related Notes of Guidance issued by the Institute of Public Relations and encourage others to do the same.

2. Fundamental to good public relations practice is:

    Integrity
    *   Honest and responsible regard for the public interest;

    *   Checking the reliability and accuracy of information before dissemination;

    *   Never knowingly misleading clients, employers, employees, colleagues and fellow professionals about the nature of representation or what can be competently delivered and achieved;

    *   Supporting the IPR Principles by bringing to the attention of the IPR examples of malpractice and unprofessional conduct.

Competence

- Being aware of the limitations of professional competence: without limiting realistic scope for development, being willing to accept or delegate only that work for which practitioners are suitably skilled and experienced;

- Where appropriate, collaborating on projects to ensure the necessary skill base.

Transparency and conflicts of interest

- Disclosing to employers, clients or potential clients any financial interest in a supplier being recommended or engaged;

- Declaring conflicts of interest (or circumstances which may give rise to them) in writing to clients, potential clients and employers as soon as they arise;

- Ensuring that services provided are costed and accounted for in a manner that conforms to accepted business practice and ethics.

Confidentiality

- Safeguarding the confidences of present and former clients and employers;

- Being careful to avoid using confidential and 'insider' information to the disadvantage or prejudice of clients and employers, or to self-advantage of any kind;

- Not disclosing confidential information unless specific permission has been granted or the public interest is at stake or if required by law.

3 Maintaining professional standards

- IPR members are encouraged to spread awareness and pride in the public relations profession where practicable by, for example:

  - Identifying and closing professional skills gaps through the Institute's Continuous Professional Development programme;

  - Offering work experience to students interested in pursuing a career in public relations;

  - Participating in the work of the Institute through the committee structure, special interest and vocational groups, training and networking events;

- Encouraging employees and colleagues to join and support the IPR;

- Displaying the IPR designatory letters on business stationery;

- Specifying a preference for IPR applicants for staff positions advertised;

- Evaluating the practice of public relations through use of *The IPR Toolkit* and other quality management and quality assurance systems (e.g. ISO standards); and constantly striving to improve the quality of business performance;

- Sharing information on good practice with members and, equally, referring perceived examples of poor practice to the Institute.

Reproduced with the permission of the PRCA.

PRCA Professional Charter

1 A member firm shall:

1.1 Have a positive duty to observe the highest standards in the practice of public relations. Furthermore a member has the responsibility at all times to deal fairly and honestly with clients, past and present, fellow members and professionals, the public relations profession, other professions, suppliers, intermediaries, the media of communication, employees, and above all else the public. 1.2 Be expected to be aware of, understand and observe this code, any amendment to it, and any other codes which shall be incorporated into this code, and to remain up-to-date with the content and recommendations of any guidance or practice papers issued by the PRCA, and shall have a duty to conform to good practice as expressed in such guidance or practice papers. 1.3 Uphold this code and co-operate with fellow members in so doing by enforcing decisions on any matter arising from its application. A member firm that knowingly causes or permits a member of its staff to act in a manner inconsistent with this code is party to such action and shall itself be deemed to be in breach of it. Any member of staff of a member company who acts in a manner inconsistent with this code must be disciplined by the employer. A member firm shall not: 1.4 Engage in any practice nor be seen to conduct itself in any manner detrimental to the reputation of the Association or the reputation and interests of the public relations profession.

2   Conduct towards the public, the media and other professionals

A member firm shall:

2.1 Conduct its professional activities with proper regard to the public interest. 2.2 Have a positive duty at all times to respect the truth and shall not disseminate false or misleading information knowingly or recklessly, and to use proper care to avoid doing so inadvertently. 2.3 Have a duty to ensure that the actual interest of any organisation with which it may be professionally concerned is adequately declared. 2.4 When working in association with other professionals, identify and respect the codes of these professions and shall not knowingly be party to any breach of such codes. 2.5 Cause the names of all its directors, executives and retained consultants who hold public office, are members of either House of Parliament, are members of Local Authorities or of any statutory organisation or body, to be recorded in the relevant section of the PRCA Register. 2.6 Honour confidences received or given in the course of professional activity. 2.7 Neither propose nor undertake any action which would constitute an improper influence on organs of government, or on legislation, or on the media of communication. 2.8 Neither offer nor give, nor cause a client to offer or give, any inducement to persons holding public office or members of any statutory body or organisation who are not directors, executives or retained consultants, with intent to further the interests of the client if such action is inconsistent with the public interest.

3   Conduct towards clients

A member firm shall:

3.1 Safeguard the confidences of both present and former clients and shall not disclose or use these confidences, to the disadvantage or prejudice of such clients or to the financial advantage of the member firm, unless the client has released such information for public use, or has given specific permission for its disclosure; except upon the order of a court of law. 3.2 Inform a client of any shareholding or financial interest held by that firm or any member of that firm in any company, firm or person whose services it recommends. 3.3 Be free to accept fees, commissions or other valuable considerations from persons other than a client, only provided such considerations are disclosed to the client. 3.4 Shall list the names of its clients in the Annual Register of the Association. 3.5 Be free to negotiate with a client terms that take into account factors other than hours worked and seniority of staff involved. These special factors, which are also applied by other professional advisers, shall have regard to all the circumstances of the specific situation and in particular to: (a) The complexity of the issue, case, problem or assignment, and the difficulties associated with its completion. (b) The professional or specialised skills and the seniority levels of staff engaged, the time spent and the degree of responsibility involved. (c) The amount of documentation necessary to be perused or prepared, and its importance. (d) The place and circumstances where the assignment is carried out in whole or in part. (e) The scope, scale and value of the task, and its importance as an issue or project to the client. A member firm shall not: 3.6 Misuse information regarding its client's business for financial or other gain. 3.7 Use inside information for gain. Nor may a consultancy, its members or staff directly invest in their clients' securities without the prior written permission of the client and of the member's chief executive or chief financial officer or compliance officer. 3.8 Serve a client under terms or conditions which might impair its independence, objectivity or integrity. 3.9 Represent conflicting or competing interests without the express consent of the clients concerned. 3.10 Guarantee the achievement of results which are beyond the member's direct capacity to achieve or prevent. 3.11 Invite any employee of a client advised by the member to consider alternative employment; (an advertisement in the press is not considered to be an invitation to any particular person).

4   **Conduct towards colleagues**

A member firm shall:

4.1 Adhere to the highest standards of accuracy and truth, avoiding extravagant claims or unfair comparisons and giving credit for ideas and words borrowed from others. 4.2 Be free to represent its capabilities and services to any potential client, either on its own initiative or at the behest of the client, provided in so doing it does not seek to break any existing contract or detract from the reputation or capabilities of any member consultancy already serving that client. A member firm shall not: 4.3 Injure the professional reputation or practice of another member.

5   **Discriminatory conduct**

A member is required to take all reasonable care that professional duties are conducted without causing offence on the grounds of gender, race, religion, disability or any other form of discrimination or unacceptable reference.

Appendix 4:
Glossary

AA	Advertising Association
ABC	Audit Bureau of Circulation
ACORN	A Classification Of Residential Neighbourhoods
Account	An organisation which subcontracts some or all of its public relations function to a public relations consultancy becomes an account within the consultancy
Account team	For each account there is an account team, which may consist of a board director, account director, account manager and account executive or a combination of these, depending on the size and complexity of the account
Ad hoc (Lat)	Impromptu, improvised, for a specific occasion – in PR often refers to project work subcontracted to a consultancy when in-house resources are limited
Advertorial	Paid for space, copy written and art directed by the publication so that it fits house style, carrying information about a product or service
AIDA	Acronym for the four stages of response to communication – Attention, Interest, Desire and Action
ASA	Advertising Standards Authority
Audience	The people you want to reach with your PR messages. You may have more than one and some may be very discrete groups, perhaps numbering less than ten individuals
Audit	Research and the analysis of that research
AVE	Advertising Value Equivalents – the measurement of a size of a piece of media coverage (column inches, seconds on TV, radio) and working out how much it is worth based on what it would have cost to buy as advertising space – pretty much discredited as a way of evaluating PR effect

Awareness	An important measurement which tells how many of your target audiences know about and understand your organisation, product or service. You can measure both unprompted awareness (e.g. Give me the names of major high street banks) and prompted awareness (e.g. Have you heard of the following – Abbey National, Barclays, Nat West…?). This measure can be used at the beginning and end of a PR campaign to help determine its success against objectives
BARB	Broadcasters' Audience Research Bureau
Beta (digibeta)	The Broadcast quality tape, used for corporate videos, video news releases etc.
BRAD	British Rate and Data – a directory which provides information about media within the UK
Benchmark	A first measure of what is happening now, which subsequent measures can be compared with, to evaluate the effect of public relations activities. Can also mean best practice
Brand manager	Person responsible for decision making about a brand
Broadsheets	The serious daily and Sunday newspapers, like *The Times* and *The Guardian*, printed on large page format. Contrast with tabloids like *The Mail* and *The Sun*. All broadsheets now have websites too
B2B	Business-to-business, a specific type of approach to PR, where the target is the business audience
B2C	Business-to-consumer
By-line	The name of the author of an article or news story, which appears just below the headline. Some pieces are attributed to an unnamed correspondent or a news agency

Campaign	A series of coordinated PR tactics designed to achieve a specific objective over a specific timescale
CAM	The Communication, Advertising and Marketing Education Foundation – the examining board for public relations, advertising and marketing
Caption	The text that goes with the photo or illustration. Fixed to the reverse of the image. Should include name, e-mail address and telephone number of the sender. If a photo is transmitted electronically the caption should be embedded in the image and included on the e-mail
Centrespread	The middle pages of a journal that open out flat and permit greater scope for creativity
CIM	Chartered Institute of Marketing
Circulation	The number of copies a publication prints and sells (i.e. the number of copies in circulation). This figure is usually considered alongside the readership figure to give a complete picture of the title's reach and strength
Client	An organisation which has employed a PR consultancy to work on its behalf – also refers to the individual(s) – the clients – who manage the contract between the client and consultancy
Clip	Short piece of film, videotape or audiotape
Column inches/centimetres	Used to measure quantity, rather than quality, of press coverage
Columnist	Writer with a regular slot in a newspaper or magazine, which carries their name and often a photograph. These days many have a background in entertainment, the arts, sport or politics rather than straight journalism

Communications audit	Research study, focusing on how an organisation communicates with its target audiences and how those target audiences currently perceive the organisation
Consumer PR	Public relations programmes that focus on consumers, as purchasers and users of a product or service, as the central target audience. These types of programmes often include product launches, advertorials, reader offers, competitions, awards and so on (see chapter eleven)
Contact report	The notes from a meeting between client and consultancy which capture the action points. Usually written by the account executive and circulated ideally no later than 24 hours after the meeting
Controlled circulation	Publications which are distributed free of charge to a defined list of recipients
Copy	Usually means the text, the written word. It is also the words on an advertisement. In advertising and in printing it specifically means all the material that will be printed – both words and pictures
Copy date	The deadline by which material must reach a publication if it is to be included in the next edition. Miss the copy date and the page will be blank
Copyright	In a nutshell, the right to use a piece of creative work. Usually resides with the creator – the writer, photographer or illustrator – unless different contractual terms are agreed. Intellectual property is also an issue particularly when a consultancy or agency develops concepts on a client's behalf and should be credited accordingly

Corporate identity	The logo, typeface, corporate colours and other design elements that are adopted by an organisation which make it unique and recognisable
Corporate PR	Public relations programmes that focus on influencers, brokers, analysts and opinion formers – and sometimes the general public too – in order to generate a favourable opinion towards an organisation. These types of programmes often include special events, facility visits, sponsorships, the production of literature and branded products, advertorials, website development, management and so on (see chapter eleven)
Correspondent	A journalist with a specialism – education, foreign affairs, media and so on – who may build a strong reputation as a leading expert on the subject
Cost per thousand	The cost of reaching 1,000 members of a target audience using a particular medium – enables media to be cost compared
Coverage	The quantity and quality of media space achieved by the public relations effort
Crisis/crisis PR	Dictionary definitions describe a crisis as a 'crucial stage or turning point', 'an unstable period especially one of extreme trouble, suspense or danger'. In public relations terms, a crisis is usually understood to be 'a serious incident affecting, for example, human safety, the environment, and/or product or corporate reputation and which has either received or been threatened by adverse publicity' (see chapter eleven)
Cut/cutting	A piece of press coverage
Cyberspace	The online world and its communication networks – originally coined by William Burroughs
Database marketing	Use of computers to profile and contact customers

Day book	Term used by some PR practitioners for the note-books they use to record notes from meetings, telephone conversations, activities and tasks relating to their work – provides a useful record and is helpful in terms of planning and organising, especially when multi-tasking
Dealer/delivery partner relations	A PR programme that focuses dealers or partners as the main stakeholder group or target audience. These types of programmes may include seminars, workshops and training events, conferences and exhibitions, incentive schemes, awards and competitions, newsletters and so on
Demographics	The study and definition of population structure
Desk research	Research using already available information from a wide variety of sources. May include past press coverage, market reports and research, opinion polls, reference works, past papers etc.
DTP	Desk Top Publishing – literally the ability to produce copy on your PC or Mac using software and sending it electronically to the printer – a fast and cost-effective way to produce newsletters, house journals, leaflets and other printed materials
Direct response	Material which includes a website address or telephone number and invites recipients to contact the organisation direct
e-journalists	Journalists working on e-media
e-media	Online media
e-media relations	Communications with journalists online
e-press release	News release delivered by e-mail
e-PR	Electronic public relations
e-zines	Interactive online magazines

Embargo	Instruction not to print/broadcast a story before a particular time and date. Useful when dealing with an advance issue of a speech or report. Also used when international time differences may be an issue
Evaluation	One of the biggest issues in PR – the qualitative and quantitative measurement of PR effectiveness
Event management	The professional planning, development and execution of events which have a PR purpose (see chapter thirteen)
Exclusive	A story given to one publication. Fine for features, not used for 'real' news stories. When involving celebrities is a pretty strong indicator that the story may have been paid for by the paper
Expenses	Costs associated with the execution of the PR programme and which are paid for by the client or employer. These include travelling, accommodation, food and drink, entertaining and hospitality
Extranet	Private computer network facilitating interactive communications with third parties on a need to know basis
Facility visit	A educational trip for journalists or for a small party of influential opinion formers for the purposes of generating media coverage, improving levels of understanding, providing reassurance after a crisis and so on
Feature	PR features are usually discussed and agreed with the editor and written to a brief

Fee	The payment made to a consultancy or agency for time spent on the account. There are three main types of fee – agreed retainer fees, normally the same amount, paid every month, based on an average of time spent over the year; project fees, which are agreed in advance and which may be paid in advance or 50% in advance and 50% on completion of the project; or ad hoc fees, where fees are charged based on the actual time spent that month and which may therefore vary from one month to the next
Financial PR	Public relations programmes that focus on the financial institutions, brokers and analysts as the central target audience. These types of programmes often include the publication of annual and interim reports and accounts, the announcement of mergers and acquisitions, flotations and so on (see chapter eleven)
Five Ws	Who, What, Where, When and Why? Questions which must be answered by every press release
FMCG	Fast Moving Consumer Goods
Focus groups	A qualitative research technique. Small groups (usually 4-12 people) run by a market researcher, for the purposes of understanding current perceptions and attitudes and testing new concepts prior to launch. Groups may be representative of any stakeholder group – staff, opponents, supporters, dealers, opinion formers, indeed any group whose opinion is important in the development of the PR strategy
Freelance	Self-employed public relations professionals, writers, artists, researchers and photographers, who are called in to take on projects for clients and consultancies alike. There is enormous growth in freelance with portfolio working and people adjusting their own work/life balance

Ghost writer	Writer who writes material for someone else, which appears as if written by that individual
Grapevine	The process whereby information – largely based on rumour – is informally spread from one person to another
Hard news	AKA real news, which is focused on people and events as opposed to business or organisational news
ICO	International Committee of Public Relations Consultancies Associations Ltd
Informal research	Gathering statistically insignificant information which may add new perspective, creative thought, new views, colour and insight in the planning process – includes product testing, store checks, talking heads, anecdote and off the record discussions with small samples
Image	The combined impression target audiences have about your organisation, based on what they think, know and feel
ILR	Independent Local Radio
Influencer	An individual who has the influence to affect stakeholders' opinions about an organisation
In-house	An internal department managing and/or implementing its own public relations using its own staff
Input	1) The initial research and fact finding stages in the PR planning process
	2) The input into the PR programme – e.g. press releases, literature, speeches etc.
	3) Has sometimes been used to mean client input into the PR campaign which enables a consultancy to do its job and make the appropriate output (in this context almost a contractual issue)

Internet	Global public network of computers
Intranet	Internal and private computer network facilitating internal communications
IPR	Institute of Public Relations
IPRA	International Public Relations Association
ISBA	Incorporated Society of British Advertisers
ISDN	Integrated Systems Digital Network – digital telecommunications lines which permit electronic data transmission – also used to send and receive photographs, audio and video to news intake desks
ISP	Institute of Sales Promotion
ITC	Independent Television Commission
ITN	Independent Television News
JIC…	Joint Industry Committees…
JICNAR	…for National Readership Surveys
JICPAR	…for Posters
RAJAR	…Radio
JICTAR	…Television
JICCAR	…Cable
	(NB Correct at time of writing. However with convergence and a review of regulation in media these committees may be replaced and new regulatory bodies formed which better reflect the needs of the industry today.)
Junk mail	Direct mail that is immediately binned, judged as being irrelevant by the reader
Livery	The use of the corporate identity on an organisation's vehicles e.g. lorries, planes, train carriages etc.

Lobby correspondent	A journalist who is given access to parts of the Palace of Westminster not open to the public – hence he/she mixes with MPs, Ministers and politicos and is permitted to report 'off the record' statements from unnamed sources at the heart of government
Lobbyist	Represents a third party and seeks to make that party's cause known to MPs, Ministers and civil servants often to effect changes to legislation etc.
MRS	Market Research Society
Marketing	'The management process responsible for identifying, anticipating and satisfying customers' requirements profitably' (Chartered Institute of Marketing)
Marketing communications	Sometimes abbreviated to MarComms – a catch-all term for the range of materials and techniques used to communicate with the market – from sales brochures, leaflets, and business cards through to advertising and after-sales service
Marketing mix	The cocktail of elements that make up the marketing strategy
Media evaluation	'The systematic appraisal (often using computer models) of how an organisation, its products and services or those of its competitors are reported in the media' (*Michael Fairchild*). Many specialist companies undertake this sort of evaluation; the simplest analysis can be done by the PR practitioner, perhaps using specially designed software
Media relations	The management of the flow of news to and enquiries from the media
Monitoring	Observing and recording broadcast media
Netiquette	Good manners when using e-mail and corresponding within newsgroups and chatrooms

News agencies	Organisations which gather and distribute news. The Press Association and Reuters are the best known. Two-Ten Communications also distributes company news
Niche market	A specific, small but unified target audience or stakeholder group
'No comment'	Never say it! Suggests avoidance and even guilt
NPA	Newspaper Publishers Association
'Off-the-record'	Never say it – unless you are prepared for the information you give to be published. Consider any information given to a journalist to be in the public domain
Objectives	Used almost interchangeably with goals and aims. An objective defines what PR is setting out to achieve. Objectives should always be SMART (Specific, Measurable, Achievable, Realistic and Timed). An example might be – to be recognised by 2005 as the leading authority on epilepsy in the UK among health professionals
Omnibus surveys	An existing market survey – among 1,000-2,000 people, representative of a target audience – which an organisation can piggy back and use to ask questions. A fast cost-effective way to obtain simple information for PR planning or to generate material for a media release. By phone and face-to-face and increasingly online via e-mail
OTS/OTH	Opportunities to see/hear – derived from advertising measurement, the number of times the target audience could potentially view or hear the organisation's messages
Outcome	'The degree to which public relations activity has changed people's opinions, attitudes or behaviour' (*Michael Fairchild*)

Output	'The simplest form of measurement, which records the production of the PR effort (media analysis of press materials issues, numbers attending events etc.) (*Michael Fairchild*)
Out-take	'The degree to which the target audience is aware of the message, has retained and understood it' (*Michael Fairchild*)
PPA	Periodical Publishers Association
PRCA	Public Relations Consultants Association
PRE	Planning, research and evaluation
Panels	A group of people, who take part in continuous research and are interviewed several times over a period of months or years
Penetration	A percentage measure indicating what proportion of the target audience bought a product
Photo agency	Like a news agency but supplies news photos to press and others. Now fully digital
Pilots	Effectively putting a new idea into a small test market to see how it is understood by the target audience and to refine the idea before it is introduced to a wider audience
Plan	The framework for the PR activity – the tactics outlined in a coherent whole
Polls	Large scale simple surveys which gain mass opinion on a defined subject. Undertaken by specialist companies. Groups surveyed may include: the general public, the police force, army, healthcare professionals and parents. The micro sample is usually selected to reflect the macro group

Pre-test	Checking that new messages and concepts will prompt the desired out-take among the stake-holders before the material is shown to the general public
Press office	A central resource for journalists within an organisation. 'Real' press offices are now comple-mented by 'virtual' press offices online
Press kit	Pack of material created for journalists to support a news release
Press release	News story written by a public relations prac-titioner for an organisation
Primary research	New and original data, commissioned by the interested organisation
Product manager	Person responsible for a product type
Programme	The detailed PR plan, which is often long-term (one, two, three years or longer) and is designed to be on strategy and to meet the set objectives
Publics	Rather archaic term meaning target audiences or stakeholders
Qualitative research	Research which will look in-depth at people's attitudes, opinions, prejudices, beliefs and responses. Helps give a rounded view and may dismiss an organisation's long held or incorrect self-perceptions
Quantitative research	Research undertaken with a representative sample of the target audience delivering numer-ical data
Relationship marketing	Approach which concentrates on the long-term relationship between an organisation and its stakeholders
Reputation management	The main task of public relations

SWOT	Strengths, Weaknesses, Opportunities, Threats – factors used in situation analysis for communications and marketing purposes
Search engines	A site or the software that enables a search of information on the Internet
Segmentation	The process whereby consumers with similar needs are grouped together
Situation analysis	What is really happening here and now, defined through research and analysis
Snail mail	Regular mail compared to e-mail
Spam	Junk mail delivered online as unsolicited e-mails.
Stakeholders	Anyone who has or could have in the future a direct or indirect interest in the organisation and its activities and with whom the organisation should have open lines of communication – interchangeable with target audiences
Strategy	Many theorists have tried to define strategy. One of the most compelling definitions we can apply to PR strategy is 'the big idea' – the overarching principle governing **how** you will approach the PR programme or campaign, not what you want to achieve (the objectives) nor the details of what you will do (the tactics)
TGI	Target Group Index
Tabloids	Also called Red Tops – daily newspapers printed in a small page format with red title banners
Tactics	Specific activities which form the overall PR programme or campaign
Target audiences	See stakeholders
Tracking studies	Continuous research to identify trends
TV advisory	Press release tailored for broadcasters so it more specifically addresses their needs

Vertical press	Journals read by interested people working in a sector, one industry or a particular profession for example *Campaign* – the weekly journal for the advertising industry – is read by account executives, art directors, media planners, agency staff and clients
Viral marketing	Based on the notion that everyone on the planet is connected indirectly through six other people, the idea that marketing online is instant and highly contagious
Video News Release	or VNR – Broadcast quality video footage shot by an organisation to give to TV stations
Voucher copy	A free copy of a publication which carries an organisation's advertisement or paid for feature
Webmaster	Someone who looks after an organisation's website
World Wide Web	The software system that runs across the Internet and not the Internet itself

Are you up to date?

Ensure you keep up to date with future developments and changes in law and practice

Photocopy this page and fill in your details, then post or fax,
alternatively e-mail or telephone – details below.

☐ **YES**, please keep me informed of future updates to *The PR Practitioner's Desktop Guide* and all other relevant publications.

My name [Mr/Ms/other] _____ [initials] _____ [surname] _____

Position _____

Organisation _____

Address _____

_____

_____

_____ Post code _____

Tel: _____ Fax: _____

E-mail: _____

Telephone	**Fax**	**E-mail**	**Post**
Call Customer Services on: **020 7749 4748**	Complete and fax this form on: **020 7729 6110**	E-mail your details to: **info@thorogood.ws**	Desktop Guides Marketing 10-12 Rivington Street London EC2A 3DU

Hawksmere publishing

Hawksmere publishes a wide range of books, reports, special briefings, psychometric tests and videos. Listed below is a selection of key titles.

Other Desktop Guides

The marketing strategy desktop guide
Norton Paley   *£16.99*

Written in a clear, practical style this desktop guide gives a comprehensive understanding of the essential key tools and techniques behind any marketing strategy. It covers the management of your: markets, competitive position, customer behaviour, pricing strategies, products/services, distribution, finance and marketing opportunities.

The sales manager's desktop guide
Mike Gale and Julian Clay   *£16.99*

This book is essential reading for sales managers and everyone involved in sales in all types of organisation, large and small. This indispensible guide covers the following key issues: leadership, business planning, recruitment and selection, motivation, handling and developing people, the sales model, sales tools for the effective manager, the company culture, managing change and selling through dealers and channels.

The company director's desktop guide
David Martin   *£16.99*

This book is essential reading for all directors and professional advisers and will ensure that the reader meets their legal responsibilities, anticipates and resolves problems and works effectively with all parts of the business. The principal areas which are addressed are directors' responsibilities: formal procedures and documents, leadership and management, corporate governance, working with shareholders and public aspects of directorship. Corporate governance in the 21st century is also addressed in this detailed guide.

The credit controller's desktop guide (second edition)
Roger Mason   *£16.99*

A comprehensive guide to collecting debts effectively, this book covers all aspects of the credit controller's work. Fully up-to-date and written in a clear, practical style, the author, who has considerable experience of credit control for over 20 years, includes case studies, standard letters and forms and an update on the latest legal developments. Key issues covered include: credit control policies, legal action (principles to follow and how to achieve a satisfactory outcome through the courts), as well as factoring, credit agencies and credit insurance.

The company secretary's desktop guide
Roger Mason   *£16.99*

This is a clear comprehensive guide to the complex procedures and legislation governing effective company legislation. All aspects of the Company Secretary's work is covered including share capital, share registration and dividends; accounts and auditors; mergers and acquisitions; profit sharing and share option schemes in addition to voluntary arrangements, administration orders and receivership. This fully up-to-date, practical guide is essential reading for Company Secretaries, Directors, Administrators, Solicitors and Accountants.

The finance and accountancy desktop guide
Ralph Tiffin   *£16.99*

This book, sub-titled, A Handbook for the Non-Financial Manager, is a guide to all aspects of accounting, financial and business literacy. Each chapter is divided into two sections: section one gives a clear insight into the main areas of business and financial accounting, demystifying terms and techniques. The second section should be consulted when a deeper knowledge of that particular topic is required. Also included are examples of standard layouts, as well as review questions with feedback. Invaluable coverage is given on fundamental accounting concepts, cash flow and interpreting financial statements and using ratios, as well as costing and budgeting.

The commercial engineer's desktop guide
Tim Boyce   *£16.99*

A practical source of reference, guidance and techniques, this book shows you how to combine successful design and innovation with effective business skills and acumen. It explains legal, contractual and commercial matters in a clear and straightforward way, taking you through every stage of putting the contract together and seeing it through. There are also helpful chapters on commercial relationships and effective negotiation. Tim Boyce has held senior positions in Plessey, Siemens, British Aerospace and BAE Systems.

The training manager's desktop guide
Eddie Davies   *£16.99*

This practical book explains in detail how to develop the right training strategy and make the training productive for everyone. The topics covered include: development, the wider environment, training strategy, planning effectively, designing, writing, organising, delivering, continued professional development and how to manage the training office. Eddie Davies shares the knowledge he has gained as a human resource development specialist with over 20 years, experience.

Masters in Management

Mastering business planning and strategy
Paul Elkin £19.99

Mastering financial management
Stephen Brookson £19.99

Mastering leadership • *Michael Williams* £19.99

Mastering marketing • *Ian Ruskin-Brown* £22.00

Mastering negotiations • *Eric Evans* £19.99

Mastering people management • *Mark Thomas* £19.99

Mastering personal and interpersonal skills
Peter Haddon £16.99

Mastering project management • *Cathy Lake* £19.99

Essential Guides

The essential guide to buying and selling unquoted
companies • *Ian Smith* £29.99

The essential guide to business planning
and raising finance
Naomi Langford-Wood & Brian Salter £29.99

Business Action Pocketbooks

Edited by David Irwin

Building your business pocketbook £10.99

Developing yourself and your
staff pocketbook £10.99

Finance and profitability pocketbook £10.99

Managing and employing
people pocketbook £10.99

Sales and marketing pocketbook £10.99

Managing projects and operations
pocketbook £9.99

Effective business communications
pocketbook £9.99

PR techniques that work pocketbook
Edited by Jim Dunn £9.99

Adair on leadership pocketbook
Edited by Neil Thomas £9.99

Other titles

The John Adair handbook of management
and leadership • *Edited by Neil Thomas* £19.95

The handbook of management fads
Steve Morris £8.95

The inside track to successful management
Dr Gerald Kushel £16.95

The management tool kit • *Sultan Kermally* £10.99

Working smarter • *Graham Roberts-Phelps* £15.99

Testing management skills • *Michael Williams* £12.95

Boost your company's profits • *Barrie Pearson* £12.99

The art of headless chicken management
Elly Brewer and Mark Edwards £6.99

Telephone tactics • *Graham Roberts-Phelps* £9.99

Exploiting IT in business • *David Irwin* £12.99

EMU challenge and change – the implications
for business • *John Atkin* £11.99

Everything you need for an NVQ in management
Julie Lewthwaite £19.99

Sales management and organisation
Peter Green £9.99

Time management and personal development
John Adair and Melanie Allen £9.99

Negotiate to succeed
Edited by Julie Lewthwaite £12.99

Companies don't succeed – people do!
Graham Roberts-Phelps £12.99

Customer relationship management
Graham Roberts-Phelps £12.99

Business health check
Carol O'Connor £12.99

Hawksmere also has an extensive range of reports and special briefings which are written specifically for professionals wanting expert information.

For a full listing of all Hawksmere publications, or to order any title, please call Hawksmere Customer Services on 020 7824 8257 or fax on 020 7730 4293.